The British Expat's Guide to Grocery Shopping in America

MAXINE CLEMINSON

CONTENTS

ACKNOWLEDGMENTS

This book wouldn't have been possible without my wonderful network of family and friends.

I would particularly like to thank Tricia Gordon & Graham Harris (my Aunty and Uncle) and old University friends Fern & Ste Calvert who welcomed us to Houston and eased our transition into life in America. Your help and support during that unsettled period was invaluable.

Huge thanks are also owed to the wonderful Mums of the Cheeky Monkeys and Tots About Town playgroups here in Houston who have been an endless source of information, support and (occasionally drunken) entertainment. In no particular order I would like to thank Holly Dawkin, Louise Wilson, Helen Rashbrook, Katy Bate, Lesley Mooney, Hazel Coutts, Rebecca Farrant, Marcela Secco, Deb Giedris, Kate Vickers, Jemma Aitken, Sarah Montana, Caroline Thomas, Marianne Wallace and Stephanie Chadwick for either their direct input into the book, or their support & enthusiasm for yet another of my hare-brained schemes!

I would also like to thank Lorna Ramsay, realtor & general wonder woman, for running the invaluable and exceedingly helpful Wednesday Coffee email list… a vital source of knowledge and experience for the newly arrived expat!

The ladies of the Schlumberger Spouses Association also deserve huge thanks for their kindness and support. You are greatly appreciated!

Massive heartfelt thanks go to my family back in the UK/Malta/Lanzarote who I miss hugely. I couldn't have made the brave step of moving internationally without their unconditional love & support… or the invention of Skype!

And last, but not least, to my own family here in Houston. My darling husband, Clemmy, and the 3 bestest little boys in the world! Thank you for making my life as complete and fulfilling as it is. I love you beyond words.

1 – INTRODUCTION

In relative terms, I am a newbie to the expat scene, especially when you consider how many seasoned veterans of this lifestyle there are in Houston alone (particularly in the oil and gas industry in which my husband works)! Our move from leafy Berkshire to Texas in the spring of 2010 was my family's first international relocation and it has taken a good couple of years of living in the USA to really understand some of the big differences. After years of watching American TV and movies we felt that we 'knew' all about America and its culture. It was going to be an easy move, right? Well the answer was yes … and no. When you compare our move from the UK to America to some of the more exotic locations our fellow expats end up living, our relocation was very easy. Americans speak (mostly) the same language as us Brits, they have large well-stocked supermarkets, the schools are good, the houses (in Texas at least) are massive and you can enjoy a great quality of life. However, there are just enough cultural differences to make the transition a little bumpy at times! There are many new things to get your head around… driving an automatic on the wrong side of the road, the whole medical insurance thing with its deductibles, co-pays and various other terms you'd never heard of (and end up wishing you never had), finding a new home/school/social life and then on top of all that even the simplest things like shopping for groceries are enough to cause confusion and frustration. The huge supermarkets are a daunting experience for the newly arrived expat, with their unfamiliar products, terminology and routines.

After nearly 3 years I feel that I have acclimatised enough to be considered a reliable source of advice – at least in terms of where to shop and what to ask for! In writing my blog *A Mama With Ideas* www.mamawithideas.com, I found myself constantly providing 'translations' from American to English for the benefit of my readers in the UK, and vice versa. It was only a small leap from that to this… a dedicated guide for people making the same move as we did.

This book is written with two uses in mind: firstly, I expect there will be people who will read it in nervous anticipation of an upcoming move trying to mentally prepare for relocation. For that purpose, I have tried to include a fair bit of descriptive detail of the differences and this information is split into chapters on the main food groups. Secondly, I have created some (hopefully) useful resources aimed at easing the shopping experience of the newly arrived Brit in America – these include shopping lists for your first week, a shopping list to restock your pantry once you have a house and sources of popular items! Finally, I hope that the book will continue to be useful as a quick reference guide that can be picked up and dipped into as needed. For this purpose I have created an easy to use alphabetical index at the end.

2 – WHERE & HOW TO SHOP AND GENERALLY USEFUL TIDBITS!

America is a big place and while there are national chains of supermarkets with stores in most neighbourhoods, there are also a number of big regional chains. Here in Texas, the big grocery stores/supermarkets (with comparisons to similar ones in the UK) are:

- **Whole Foods Market** – this is a chain of stores that specializes in natural and organic foods. It prides itself on its sustainable credentials. It is comparable to Waitrose or Marks & Spencer in terms of the quality of its produce (and its prices).
- **Randalls (part of the Safeway group)** – Safeway is a national (multinational) chain of supermarkets and is well known for its upscale private brand, Safeway Select. They also carry an 'own brand' value range. It is comparable to Sainsbury's or Tesco's in the UK.
- **Kroger** – This is the largest nationwide chain of grocery stores in the US. It has a Signature private brand offering upscale products (similar to Tesco's Finest). In most Kroger stores there is a

3

section dedicated to natural or organic foods (including frozen and fresh items... look for a separate refrigerator in the 'Produce' area for organic or natural milk/cheese/butter/eggs/juices etc...). Overall, it's comparable to Tesco's or Sainsbury's.

- **H-E-B** – This is a Texan regional supermarket chain. As with Kroger & Randalls it has its own value and upscale brands (Central Market is their gourmet/high quality range). It prides itself on being a 'local' chain.

- **Walmart** – Most Brits will be familiar with this chain in the form of Asda (owned by Walmart) in the UK. It offers a lot of value and economy product ranges. The stores also carry a lot of non-food retail items like clothes, furniture, toys, gardening & DIY supplies, especially the large supercentres!

- **Target** – Many expats come to love Target. It's a bit of a weird one to define... a bit like a department store, but more like the old Woolworth's than Debenhams! The larger Super Target stores often carry groceries too. They have a range of their own value products, but is also the main stockist of **Archer Farms** products... a premium 'natural' or 'organic' brand.

Figure 1: Some of the larger grocery stores in Texas

Obviously, stores vary in quality and diversity of products even within the same chain and you will eventually develop a local favourite.

Home deliveries

All I can say is wave goodbye to your weekly **Ocado**-style grocery deliveries. I loved my weekly internet food shopping in the UK. Twenty minutes of clicking on items in my favourites list and then a day later a nice man delivered all my groceries in boxes that he carried to my kitchen, and even unpacked onto the counter! And for free... Bliss! But moving to Texas brought me swiftly back to Earth and back into the store in person. I guess it's the sheer geographic size of the cities here that makes providing internet grocery shopping uneconomic for most supermarkets. Either way, I have only discovered one supermarket that does a home delivery service here – Rice Epicurean (a grocery store chain based in Houston, Texas). However, not only does this upmarket store have prices much higher than the other stores locally, it also charges $15 to deliver!

There are other regional and national companies that deliver, but shipping/delivery costs are often high and many don't include refrigerated/frozen items. Try some of the following:

- Safeway offers home delivery from their stores with delivery costs starting from $3.95. Check their website to see if they deliver to your zip code - http://shop.safeway.com
- www.netgrocer.com – delivers nationwide with a range that includes some fresh/frozen items. As delivery is via courier, shipping costs can be quite high.
- www.peapod.com – a well-established internet grocer covering 11 metropolitan areas in the northeast.

Coupon Crazy & Loyalty cards

Americans love their coupons. And not just in the way that we Brits are a bit chuffed when we get a coupon through the post. Many Americans spend hours 'coupon clipping', and admittedly the savings can be massive if you can be bothered. While it can be a tad frustrating to be in the checkout queue behind someone with a folder full of cross-referenced and organised coupons taking forever (yes, this has happened to me), when you see them knocking 70% off their shopping bill it does make you wonder! Apparently, you can partially embrace this Americanism by making use of some of the online 'coupon clipping services'. They charge a small fee (often payable via **PayPal**) to mail you the coupons they list. Try the following:

- http://thecouponclippers.com
- http://www.couponsthingsbydede.com/
- http://www.couponmom.com/

It is also worthwhile signing up for store loyalty cards

(equivalent to the Tesco's clubcard or similar). Not only will they send you coupons, some of the stores offer points that can be redeemed against things like petrol. For example the Kroger card can earn you up to a dollar off per gallon of fuel at the pump in Shell garages... not to be sneezed at! Other stores like Randalls (Safeway) have two prices listed for some offers... the cheaper price is only available to cardholders!

Shopping Trolleys

You would have thought that this is a stupid thing to include, but strangely enough, there are noticeable differences between the US and UK when it comes to shopping trolleys. Firstly, if you refer to it as a "shopping trolley", people will think you're weird. A trolley to an American is a wheel or pulley attached to an overhead cable... think of the iconic San Francisco streetcars! In the US, a shopping trolley is called a shopping cart, basket, buggy or wagon (the first two being the most widely used).

Another issue I encountered was that there is a lack of shopping trolleys with more than one seat for young children. As a parent of young twins this was a massive problem for me initially. Some supermarkets have a few huge trolleys with a **Cozy Coupe** style car attached at the front... these have two seats (and thankfully two steering wheels). However, these are really only appropriate for older toddlers and in my experience have been quite stressful to use. You can occasionally find trolleys with the reclining baby seats, but these are rare and a lot of people with new babies resort to putting the infant car seat in the main part of the trolley.

My advice to people new to the country... if at all possible do your initial forays to the grocery store without kids in tow, even if that means going out in the evening and leaving them with Dad (or Mum). That way you will be able to check out the trolley situation in advance.

Shopping bags

Don't be scared when they offer to pack your shopping for you. This is standard practice as each till is usually manned by two people – a cashier and a packer. You won't be expected to tip but they often appreciate a quick ding on the bell they keep next to their checkout… this signals to their supervisor that they did a good job for you (my kids love doing this)!

The only frustrating part of having someone else pack your groceries is that they are ultra conservative about bag loading… there's definitely no chance of your bag splitting with too many items bulging out here in America. In some cases, it's literally one item to one bag! This is very frustrating if you're trying to cut back on your plastic waste. Thankfully most supermarkets recycle plastic bags and have a special bin in the entrance (you just have to remember to take them with you the next time). An alternative is to ask for paper bags as most stores will have a supply of these at the checkout too. Or bring your own reusable ones!

Weights, measures and handy hints

When shopping for foodstuff or following recipes in America it is important to remember that they still haven't switched to metric! Furthermore, their imperial weights and measures are slightly different to our old ones!

In the case of measuring dry weight, it is reassuring to know that an ounce and a pound are the same in the old UK Imperial system as in the US. This is convenient for measuring foodstuff, as many of us Brits still prefer to use imperial measures when cooking! For larger weights, the only difference to note is that Americans don't use stones, and their tons are only 2,000lb rather than 2,240lb as in the UK.

However, when measuring volume of liquids things become slightly different. In the UK, one fluid ounce is exactly that – 1 fl. oz. of water weighs 1 ounce. In America, things get a bit screwy! It all comes from the historic way in which volumes were measured. In the UK, they settled on calling 10lb (or 160 ounces) of water a gallon of liquid. In America, they used a system whereby a gallon was 231 cubic inches in volume. This amount of water actually weighs only 133.2 ounces. The long and short of it is that 1 US Gallon is about 5/6 that of a UK Gallon – worth remembering when comparing petrol prices. As in Britain, the US has 4 quarts, 8 pints or 32 gills in a gallon, BUT these measures are also consequently smaller. So, the Americans have 16 fluid ounces in their pint, whereas the British have 20 – worth remembering when ordering beer. And an American fluid ounce of water doesn't weigh an ounce, it weighs about 0.96 ounces! You may wish to invest in a new measuring jug if you intend to follow American recipes, but with only a 4% difference between a US & UK fluid ounce I haven't bothered and my cooking hasn't suffered!

Most American recipes call for ingredients to be measured by dry volume rather than weight. One of the first things you will want to equip your American kitchen with is a set of nested measuring cups and spoons. The thing to remember with measuring ingredients by volume is that some things like flour and sugar can be compressed to fit more in - 1 cup of sifted flour weighs about 100g, whereas 1 cup of settled flour weighs 140g! There are techniques for getting accurate measurements from cups. See http://busycooks.about.com/od/howtocook/a/howtome asure.htm for more information. Getting a direct conversion from US cups to weight (imperial or metric) is tricky, because different ingredients have different densities. There are however, some pretty handy online conversion tools. This webpage has a fairly comprehensive list:

- www.jsward.com/cooking/conversion.shtml

The volume of US measuring cups can be directly converted into metric volumes though:

1 cup = 240 ml
⅞ cup = 210ml
¾ cup = 180ml
½ cup = 120ml
⅓ cup = 80 ml
¼ cup = 60 ml
1 tsp. = 1 teaspoon = 5ml
1 tbsp. = 1 tablespoon = 15ml

Another oddity of American recipes is the description of a unit of butter as a stick. When you buy a pound of butter, inside the packaging it is actually divided into four individually wrapped 'sticks'. Therefore:

1 stick of butter = 1/4 pound
1 stick of butter = 1/2 cup
1 stick of butter = 8 tablespoons
1 stick of butter = 4 ounces
1 stick of butter = 113 grams

Finally, you may need to convert oven temperatures for cooking. The list below is a rough guide:

250°F = 130°C = Gas Mark ½
275°F = 140°C = Gas Mark 1
300°F = 150°C = Gas Mark 2
325°F = 170°C = Gas Mark 3
350°F = 180°C = Gas Mark 4
375°F = 190°C = Gas Mark 5
400°F = 200°C = Gas Mark 6
425°F = 220°C = Gas Mark 7
450°F = 230°C = Gas Mark 8
475°F = 240°C = Gas Mark 9

Storage canisters
In the UK, I didn't really worry too much about pests in the home other than my kids! In the summer, we

occasionally ended up with the odd ant invasion, but nothing particularly distressing. Here in the US, particularly here in Texas, the bugs are on a whole other level! Many people have regular pest control visit their home to spray insecticides to prevent the spiders and cockroaches from invading too much, but it is an uncomfortable fact of life living here that you will come face to face with some nasty bugs you wouldn't routinely come across in the UK. The huge tree roaches here in Texas (while different from the German cockroaches that plague dirty kitchens and bars) are still pretty revolting and they will sometimes come inside to get away from the heat outside!

After my first encounter with one of these bad boys (and I confess, I screamed like a big sissy and got a native Texan friend to rescue me) I scrubbed my whole house from top to bottom in revulsion. I also went and invested in airtight storage canisters for all loose food products, e.g. breakfast cereals, flour, sugar etc… I figured that it gave me peace of mind to know that any marauding bugs couldn't get their grubby mitts on our grub! Just saying!

Hurricane kits

This is another bizarre thing to include in a book about grocery shopping! However, many parts of the US are prone to occasional hurricanes and so this is something worth considering when stocking your pantry. When Hurricane Ike struck here in Houston in 2008, friends of ours were without water for several days and electricity for 2 long weeks. There will often only be a day or so warning of this sort of event, and in many cases this often results in panic buying in the stores and petrol stations. During the North Atlantic Hurricane season (June-November) it is worth keeping a minimum of half a tank of petrol in your car, even if it means more frequent trips to the gas station. The NOAA NHC (National Oceanic & Atmospheric Administration's National Hurricane Center) also recommends that you have a basic emergency hurricane preparedness kit containing the following things:

- Water, one gallon of water per person per day for at least three days, for drinking and sanitation (a great tip we were given by some Expat friends who'd survived a big tropical storm here in Texas is to leave out your bins and buckets after the wind has died down as there is LOTS of rain in the days following a hurricane… perfect for use in flushing toilets)!
- Food, at least a three-day supply of non-perishable food (think of things like one-pot macaroni cheese boxes, tins of soup etc…)
- Battery-powered or hand crank radio and a NOAA Weather Radio with tone alert and extra batteries for both
- Torch and extra batteries
- First aid kit
- Whistle to signal for help
- Dust mask to help filter contaminated air and plastic sheeting & duct tape to shelter in place
- Wet wipes, bin bags and plastic ties for personal sanitation
- Wrench or pliers to turn off utilities
- Manual can opener for food (don't starve looking at a tin of food you can't open!)
- Local maps
- Mobile phone with chargers, inverter or solar charger

For more information, go to the NOAA NHC website:
- www.nhc.noaa.gov/prepare/ready.php

3 – FOOD ADDITIVES AND CONTROVERSIAL INGREDIENTS

I felt I ought to include a chapter on some of the food additives and ingredients you may wish to be aware of. There is enough material on this subject to write an entire other book, so I have tried to present just the factual information about a few of the 'current' additives of concern and ones specific to the US. I'm not saying that you should or shouldn't be concerned, I just thought it worth sharing the information!

My own feelings about this topic are mixed. I am a mother to 3 boys and feel a huge responsibility to make good food choices for their sakes so I try to prepare healthy home cooked food and avoid overly processed foods, high saturated fats, high sodium and the things listed below. Thankfully, no one in our family has shown any sign of food allergies, intolerances or sensitivities so I'm not I'm overly worried on a day-to-day basis. However, I do look for ingredients on the label that I recognise rather than some ridiculous sounding chemical that I can barely say, let alone spell! Conversely, I also don't want my kids to be the only ones not to enjoy the cake at a friend's birthday party, so I take a fairly relaxed view when out and about!

A good example of my attitude to this subject is in regard to **Heinz Tomato Ketchup**. I have bought this product all my adult life, and yet when I moved to the US I absent-mindedly scanned the list of ingredients and was surprised to see High Fructose Corn syrup (HFCS, more details about this ingredient later in the chapter) in place of sugar. The full list of ingredients is:

> TOMATO CONCENTRATE FROM RED RIPE TOMATOES, DISTILLED VINEGAR, *HIGH FRUCTOSE CORN SYRUP*, CORN SYRUP, SALT, SPICE, ONION POWDER, and NATURAL FLAVORING.

The same company, bowing to consumer concern about HFCS has brought out a separate product line here in the States called **Simply Heinz Ketchup** containing:

> TOMATO CONCENTRATE FROM RED RIPE TOMATOES, DISTILLED VINEGAR, *SUGAR*, SALT, ONION POWDER, SPICE, and NATURAL FLAVORING.

It's only a minor difference in ingredients, substituting the artificially manufactured HFCS for minimally processed cane sugar, and only a few cents difference in price too. Therefore, it's a bit of a no-brainer in my book... even though I'm a bit ambivalent about the 'dangers' of HFCS I choose the more 'natural' variety every time!

Artificial growth hormones

When we moved to the US in 2010, we were told by a friend to buy only organic milk based on a story she'd heard about her friend's, neighbour's, aunt's, acquaintance's (you're following this, right?) pre-teen daughter who had "developed breasts after drinking the normal milk because of the hormones"!

While this urban myth had clearly taken off with a will of its own, there is a lot of (possibly justified) controversy about the synthetic hormones in American milk. Without wanting to scaremonger, it is no secret that American milk is banned in the European Union, Canada, Japan, Australia and New Zealand. The safety concerns come from the use of artificial growth hormones that increase milk production in dairy cows in many American dairies. It is also sometimes called recombinant bovine somatotropin (rBST) or Recombinant Bovine Growth Hormone (rbGH).

While all milk naturally contains hormones related to lactation, this genetically engineered growth hormone (rBST) stimulates the production of insulin-like growth factor 1 (IGF-1) and there is a very well established correlation between abnormally high levels of IGF-1 and increased cancer risks in humans.

To counter this rather alarming statement, I want to point out that the US Food & Drug Administration (FDA) have conducted a number of studies that show the level of IGF-1 in milk from cows treated with rBST to be in the same range as that found in normal human breast milk. The use of rBST has been approved since 1993 and the FDA states that food products from rBST-treated cows are safe for human consumption. In spite of this reassurance, there are still some consumer concerns; enough to prompt several dairies, retailers and restaurants to go rBST-free.

In line with its approval of rBST, the FDA doesn't require special labelling to show if milk products come from cows given these artificial growth hormones. However, you may see some milk and milk-products labelled "rBST-free" in an effort to meet consumer demands. In these cases, most also include an additional qualifying statement to avoid legal action from pro-rBST producers: "FDA states: No significant difference in milk from cows treated with artificial growth hormones." It is worth noting that all USDA Organic products cannot contain any genetically modified components, so by definition all organic dairy products will be free from artificial growth hormones.

They say everthing's bigger in Texas... Hats, trucks, hair and...

...udders?!

mc
2012

Food Colourings

My kids don't need any help with bouncing off the walls, so I've made a concerted effort to avoid artificial food colourings where possible even though we don't have any diagnosed sensitivities or allergies. Artificial food dyes are notorious for their association with hyperactivity and a number of other problems and people who are susceptible are accustomed to rigorously reading all food labels and avoiding the culprits. The problem arises here in the US because they use a different labelling system from the E-numbers we are used to in Britain.

In the US, there are seven artificial colourings permitted in food that are also allowed in the UK (although many British manufacturers have complied with a voluntary phase-out requested by the Food Standards Agency in 2009). I have listed them with their E-number below:

- **E102 = FD&C Yellow #5 (Tartrazine)** – this notorious 'nasty' is known to cause problems for asthmatics, as well as allergic reactions and hyperactivity in sensitive individuals.
- **E110 = FD&C Yellow #6 (Sunset Yellow FCF)** – another 'baddie' known to cause problems for asthmatics, eczema sufferers, as well as allergic reactions such as hives and hyperactivity in sensitive individuals.
- **E127 = FD&C Red #3 (Erythrosine)** – not as common as the Red #40, but with similar problems in sensitive individuals. Laboratory tests show that it can increase thyroid hormone levels and lead to hyperthyroidism.
- **E129 = F&C Red #40 (Allura Red AC)** – this red dye is the most commonly used artificial colour in the US and is found in many foods (and medicines/vitamins). It has been linked in several studies to hyperactivity and ADHD in children. There are also concerns about allergic reactions, especially for asthmatics, eczema sufferers and aspirin-sensitive people.
- **E132 = FD&C Blue #2 (Indigotine)** – a blue dye linked to breathing difficulties, nausea & vomiting in sensitive individuals
- **E133 = FD&C Blue #1 (Brilliant Blue FCF)** – this blue dye has been shown to cause problems for asthmatics and linked to other allergic reactions in sensitive people.
- **E143 = FD&C Green #3 (Fast Green FCF)** – this is the least common artificial food dye used in

the US, but has been shown to be potentially toxic & carcinogenic in laboratory tests on rodents.

The only other dyes approved for food use in the US are a bit random:

- **Citrus Red 2** – a strange one, as only permitted for use in colouring the skin of whole oranges, particularly in Florida (this dye is banned in California & Arizona where oranges are also commonly grown). There are concerns about the effects this artificial dye has had on laboratory animals.

- **Orange B** – a red dye that has not been used in the food industry for many years, although it is technically not banned. It was used for the colouring of the casings of frankfurter & hot dog sausages. It was found to be toxic to laboratory animals.

Whilst use of the colourings listed previously is endemic in the US food industry, it is interesting to note that the following 'problematic' E-numbers approved for used in the UK are banned in the USA: E122, E123, E124, E131, E142, E151, and E155.

It's also worth remembering that some people have problems with 'natural' colourings such as cochineal, carmine, caramel & annatto – these will be listed by name (rather than E-number) on the food label.

If you have any concerns about sensitivity to artificial colourings or other additives to your food, speak to your doctor for more information and check all food labels carefully.

For more information, read the following article from the Center for Science in the Public Interest:

- http://cspinet.org/new/pdf/food-dyes-rainbow-of-risks.pdf.

Information is also available from the US FDA (Food & Drug Administration):

- http://www.fda.gov/downloads/Food/FoodIngr edientsPackaging/ucm094249.pdf

Artificial sweeteners

High Fructose Corn Syrup

High Fructose Corn Syrup (HFCS), known as **glucose-fructose** syrup in the UK, is a very common sugar substitute in the US where it is used in many foods. HFCS is much sweeter than real sugar and so less is needed – it is therefore a much cheaper ingredient. The low cost of HFCS compared to sugar has made it so popular with manufacturers that it has virtually replaced table sugar in all processed foods until recent years. In contrast, it is rarely used in the UK where sugar is still used as a sweetener in many products. This difference is driven by economic policies rather than health concerns as the EU has placed a quota on the production of glucose-fructose syrup (limited to only 5% of total sugar production in an attempt to protect beet sugar farming interests in the EU).

Over the last decade HFCS has prompted a lot of controversy as several reports have indicated a link between HFCS and obesity, cardiovascular disease, diabetes and liver disease. It has also been suggested in some studies that HFCS may be a source of mercury. HFCS received bad press from nutritionists, public health officials and the media to the extent that many brands are now claiming to be 'Free from High Fructose Corn Syrup' in response to consumer demands.

Research on the health issues surrounding HFCS is inconclusive but if you are concerned you can look for the presence of high fructose corn syrup on food labels and avoid it.

Aspartame

While **saccharin** was always a bit suspect due to fears of carcinogenic properties, currently it is aspartame (also known by the brand name **NutraSweet**) that is considered the controversial artificial sweetener. The safety of aspartame has been the subject of many studies and political debates, but remains approved by the US FDA with a caveat for people with phenylketonuria, a rare inherited disease that prevents phenylalanine (a breakdown product of aspartame) from being properly metabolised. Consequently, all products containing aspartame are required by the FDA to carry the warning "Phenylketonurics: Contains Phenylalanine".

While rumours persist that aspartame is carcinogenic and linked to several other diseases and disorders, the experts continue to declare it safe for use. Of more concern to medical experts is the link suggested in recent studies between artificial sweeteners and obesity (the case argued is that artificial sweeteners don't cause the same insulin response in the blood as real sugar and so the body craves more calories than is necessary).

In response to the negative press surrounding aspartame, two other brands have gained increasing popularity – sucralose (under the brand name **Splenda**) and the natural plant-derived stevia (under the brand name **Truvia**).

Artificial Flavourings

MSG

Monosodium glutamate (MSG) is a commonly used flavour-enhancer that has been scrutinised for its safety amid a number of concerns, chiefly the so-called "Chinese restaurant syndrome" whose symptoms include migraines, upset stomach, asthma and heart irregularities. MSG is the manufactured form of glutamic acid, an amino acid that helps stimulate the savoury receptors in the taste buds. As with aspartame, there are also reports suggesting a link between MSG and obesity.

The evidence for safety issues is inconclusive and the FDA reports suggest that MSG is "safe when consumed at usual levels by the general public"... a bit of a wishy-washy statement that doesn't really engender much confidence, in my opinion.

Since 2003 the FDA stipulated that when artificial MSG is added to a food it must be listed as such. However, if you are concerned about the presence of MSG in your food you need to look out for the vague 'natural flavorings' listed on some labels. This is because glutamic acid is commonly found in food sources such as tomatoes and soy sauce. Because of lack of regulation, it is impossible to determine what percentage of 'natural flavor' is actually glutamic acid. Check for products marked MSG-free if you are concerned.

Diacetyl
Diacetyl is a butter-flavouring chemical used most commonly in microwave popcorn, a popular snack in America. It first gained notoriety a few years ago when workers in several factories that manufacture this artificial butter flavouring were diagnosed with bronchiolitis obliterans, a rare and serious disease of the lungs, rather unfortunately nicknamed "popcorn worker's lung".

However, in August 2012 a consumer called Wayne Watson was awarded $7.2 million in damages by a jury who decided that his lung disease was caused by the diacetyl in microwave popcorn... the fact that the man ate 3 whole bags per day for several years prior to his diagnosis notwithstanding, it was deemed that the manufacturer and the grocery store that sold it should have warned him of the dangers!

In response, many popcorn brands are now declaring themselves "diacetyl-free" but check the label if you have concerns.

Potassium Bromate

Potassium bromate can be used as a flour improver allowing better rising of the dough. Under the right conditions, it will be completely used up in the baking of the bread. However, if too much is added or the baking temperature is not high enough, a residual amount will remain and can be harmful (bromate is considered a carcinogen). Consequently, it is banned from use in the EU and several other countries. In the US, it is still allowed, although since 1991 the FDA has urged bakers to stop using it. It is worth noting that products with the USDA Organic seal must be un-bromated, and many brands including Pepperidge Farm, Arnold, Pillsbury, Orowheat, Entenmann's & King Arthur are committed to using un-bromated flour. Check for bromated flour or potassium bromate on the label if you are concerned but it is quite rare to see these days

Trans-fats

The consumption of trans-fats (partially hydrogenated vegetable oils) has been demonstrated to lower levels of good cholesterol and so has been linked to increased risk of coronary disease. Some studies have also indicated links between consumption of trans-fats and other non-cardiovascular problems, including Alzheimer's disease, cancer, diabetes, obesity, liver dysfunction, depression and female infertility.

Since 2003, the US FDA (Food and Drug Administration) has required manufacturers to list trans-fats on the Nutrition Facts panel of foods and some dietary supplements. However, unlike in many other countries, trans-fat levels of less than 0.5 grams per serving can be listed as zero grams trans-fat on the food label. There is also no requirement to list trans-fats on institutional food packaging – the bulk packaged foods often purchased by schools, hospitals and cafeterias. However, in some cities and states additional regulations on the use of trans-fats have been implemented, for example trans-fats are banned from all restaurants in California.

Furthermore, some major food chains and manufacturers have chosen to remove or reduce trans-fats in their products and these will be labelled clearly (although as mentioned already, products can claim 0g trans-fats as long as there is <0.5 grams per serving).

4 – PRODUCE SECTION (A.K.A. FRUIT & VEG BIT)

The aim of section 1 was to give a flavour of the shopping experience in the US and a heads-up on some of the food additives/issues to be aware of… forewarned is forearmed and all that!   But the main purpose of this book is to provide assistance with navigating grocery stores in the US. So the next section (chapters 4-15) does exactly that.   Each chapter covers a main food group or topic and you will find examples and recommendations of products as well as a 'translation' where necessary!

The 'Produce' section of a US supermarket (pronounced "PRO-duce" emphasising the O rather than "PROD-uce" as we Brits would say) is where the fresh fruits and vegetables are to be found, but why they can't call it the "Fruit & Veg" section *à la* a British supermarket, I don't know?   The main differences between the US & UK is the names for things.   Obviously, the different climate, especially here in Texas, also means that the seasonal availability of certain fruits & veg are different and/or longer.

Organic fruits & vegetables are widely available.   The

United States Department of Agriculture (USDA) manages a National Organic Program (NOP) which aims to ensure the integrity of organic products in the US. It has a regulatory role, providing accreditation to producers and manufacturers of organic products. To summarise the USDA definition, organic food must be produced through approved methods that integrate cultural, biological, and mechanical practices that foster cycling of resources, promote ecological balance, and conserve biodiversity. Synthetic fertilizers, sewage sludge, irradiation, and genetic engineering may not be used. Food that has been certified organic by the USDA will carry the USDA Organic seal.

Figure 2: The USDA Organic Seal

Vegetables & salad

- **Potatoes** – you would assume that a spud, is a spud, but it's all in the variety (apparently)! And here in the US, the most common variety of potato by far, is the Idaho-grown Russet. It's a large, longish potato, with a slightly rough brown skin, but it's a good all-rounder for baking, roasting, boiling and mashing. It's also in season all year round. The potatoes we Brits are used to are often called 'gold' because of the thin, pale yellow skins. New potatoes are less easy to come by and are generally expensive. They call them 'baby' potatoes!

- **Parsnips & leeks** – both of these vegetables are not hugely popular in the USA, particularly parsnips! However, you will find them in the occasional supermarket ... hilariously, the checkout staff are usually totally bemused and have to ask you what veggie it is so they can look the code up on the till!

- **Cucumber** – the usual cucumbers available in the US are different to the ones we Brits are familiar with. They have much thicker skins, a slightly less sweet taste and contain larger, more obvious seeds than the variety we are used to in Britain. However, some supermarkets do stock *'English Seedless Cucumbers'*, which is factually incorrect, as they DO have seeds; they're just smaller and less prominent! Another difference is that the English ones come wrapped in plastic to prevent water loss (through the thinner skins), whereas the American ones are uncovered. Something to note is that most standard American varieties (including organic) have their skins waxed to make them look shinier and more appealing … it is therefore recommended to peel them, unlike the British ones which you don't need to.

Generally speaking you'll be able to find most vegetables you would find in a British supermarket. However, in some cases you will be totally confused by the different names for the same vegetable… this becomes even more difficult if you have to ask for the whereabouts of something specific, so it's worth genning up in advance to avoid any confusion:

- **Arugula** = Rocket
- **Beets** = Beetroot
- **Chicory** = Endive
- **Eggplant** = Aubergine
- **Fava beans** = Broad beans
- **Large squash or zucchini** = Marrow
- **Navy beans** = Haricot beans
- **Romaine lettuce** = Cos lettuce

- **Rutabaga** = Swede (or occasionally turnips too)
- **Scallions or green onions** = Spring onion
- **Snow peas** = Mange tout
- **String beans** = Runner beans
- **Whole kernel corn** = Sweet corn
- **Zucchini** = Courgette

Fruit

As with vegetables, the selection of fruits available is comparable to a UK supermarket, although certain fruits such as avocados and melons are a lot more popular than in Britain, especially here in Texas. One thing to note is that American's do not use the term 'punnet' for the container in which fruits or vegetables are stored – I caused major confusion in a grocery store when I asked where the punnets of strawberries were! You will often find the containers referred to by the volume instead, so a "pint of blueberries" instead of a punnet (remember a US pint is only 16oz not 20oz as in the UK). You can also use the term 'basket' or 'box' instead.

Fresh 'Erbs

Apart from the American inability to pronounce the 'h' in herb, you will find that most supermarkets stock a wide range of fresh herbs as you would expect to find in the UK! The one thing that confuses a lot of Brits new to America is the abundance of the herb cilantro in recipes and on the shelves! This was an herb I had never heard of and it confused me greatly until I picked up a bunch in the fresh herb section and took a whiff*... cilantro IS coriander!!!* However, this name change is only applicable to the fresh leaves... coriander seeds are still coriander seeds. Confused?! Me too!

5 – DAIRY

Whether you chose to be cautious and avoid dairy products with artificial growth hormones or not, there are a number of differences between the dairy products available in the US and those we Brits are used to. The following sections provide more details.

Milk

Milk. Huh? You'd have thought milk is milk. However, as with a lot of things, it's all in the name. Give it a different nomenclature and we're stuffed! I was flummoxed initially by the array of milk (and cream) available... where was my standard semi-skimmed!? However, a bit of trial and error has allowed me to draw up a comparison list so you'll be able to select the milk product you need:

- **Clotted Cream** – Not available fresh. A pasteurized version in a jar manufactured by the **Devon Cream Company** is sometimes available in the International aisle of your supermarket or online.
- **Extra thick double cream** – You can sometimes

find **Extra Heavy Cream**, but it's not very common.

- **Double cream** – The same as **Heavy** (sometimes 'Heavy whipping') cream
- **Whipping cream** – The same in the UK & US.
- **Single Cream** – Rarely seen. Sometimes you will see **Light or 'Lite' Cream**.
- **Half-and-half** – No obvious English equivalent, this is cream that is somewhere between whole milk and single cream… often used for coffee.
- **Whole Milk (3.5% fat)** – The same in the UK & US.
- **Semi Skimmed (1.8%)** – The closest equivalent in the US is **2% or Reduced Fat Milk.**
- **The One' or 1%** - Called **1%** or simply **Low Fat Milk.**
- **Skimmed Milk (0.5% fat)** – Called **Skim, Fat-free** or **Non-fat Milk.**

The brands vary by state, but popular ones include **Borden** and **Horizon Organics.** However, most supermarkets have their own range of milk products, including organic.

Butter

Butter in the US is predominantly called 'sweet cream' butter and is available in either salted or unsalted varieties. This is the same as the standard butter we are used to in the UK. You will also see varieties of cultured butter like those you get on the European continent, e.g. **President Butter** from France. These are often labelled 'European-style butter'.

As in Britain, there are a number of spreadable butter and butter substitutes, some of which are familiar brands such as **I Can't Believe It's Not Butter!** and **Benecol.** Another popular brand is **Country Crock.** A less common brand worth a try is **Earth Balance** – I particularly like their 'whipped' spread.

Because of increasing concerns about the trans-fats in such spreads, "whipped butter" is popular alternative to margarine type spreads. This is butter with a straight-from-the-fridge spreadable consistency created by aerating the butter with harmless nitrogen gas (not normal air which would encourage rancidity) rather than chemically modifying the butter's fat. A popular brand of 'whipped butter' is **Land O Lakes**. I personally find them tasty but not all that spreadable straight from the fridge.

Cheese

Most American's think that cheese is an individually packaged slice of plastic processed nonsense. You can even buy cheese in a spray can here! While a slice of processed cheese is okay on the occasional burger at a barbeque, this is not cheese in the British notion of the word. The mainstream cheese section of most US supermarkets contains nothing but packs of these cheese 'singles' or bags of pre-grated ('shredded') cheese. The main manufacturer of these is **Kraft** and they tend to be very mild and not to most Brits' palate.

To get cheeses that you recognize, you will have to look for the specialist or 'Artisan' cheese section. This is usually a deli counter near the Produce or Bakery. Expect the decent cheese to be expensive as it is imported, however, you can usually get some fairly decent American Cheddar – **Cabot** is a popular brand. Just make sure it's 'Sharp' (this adjective is the same as 'Mature' in the UK). American sharp cheddar is equivalent to a medium strength one in the UK! You can also obtain a selection of decent European cheese like Brie, Emmenthal, Gouda, Camembert, Gruyere etc… but again you will have to spend a little more. Well worth it when you consider the standard American cheeses available.

Yoghurt (or *Yogurt)*

There are a wide variety of individual yoghurt brands available (full and low-fat), including ones familiar to Brits such as **Activia**. There is also Greek yogurt (plain and flavoured) widely available. The main difficulty I had when moving to America was sourcing familiar yoghurts for my little ones. My toddlers loved the **Yoplait Petit Filous** and **Frubes** available in the UK and it took me a long time to find an alternative that suited them. As with plain Fromage Frais, this type of 'yoghurt' (okay, it's technically a cheese) is virtually impossible to obtain. I have been recently surprised to find own-brand **Petit Suisse** 'yoghurts', children's fruit flavoured fromage frais, in my local supermarket and they are good, if not identical to the beloved Petit Filous from the UK. Most children's yoghurts are low-fat and I struggled to find a whole milk variety. Brands to try include:

- **Stonyfield Organic** - This company does a range of great baby and kids yoghurts, including **YoBaby** Whole Milk Yogurts (in plain or fruit flavoured varieties) – great for babies. My boys also made the switch to **YoKids** and **YoKids Squeezers** from their beloved **Petit Filous** and **Frubes** quite easily!
- **Brown Cow** – This Company have a wide range of 'all natural' yoghurts, including whole milk, low-fat and fat free, plus Greek yoghurts.

Eggs

Not strictly dairy, I know, but often lumped under the same category. The biggest difference is that eggs in the US often have white shells! Rest assured that this doesn't alter the taste and texture; apparently it is linked to the breed and colour of the chicken! However, if you want brown eggs they are readily available … they will be clearly labelled on the box.

Differences in labelling are again worth noting. Rather than 'free range', you will often see eggs described as 'cage free'. To be labelled cage free, the U.S. Department of Agriculture (USDA) requires only that the bird spends part of its time outside. You might also come across the label 'barn-roaming' – this describes eggs that are laid by chickens that do not range freely but are confined to a barn instead of a more restrictive cage.

Other:

- **Cottage cheese** – widely available.
- **Ricotta cheese** – widely available.
- **Cream cheese** – **Philadelphia** is a popular brand here in the US.
- **Crème Fraîche** – rare, but occasionally seen in the deli sections of more upmarket supermarkets (near the fresh pasta/hummus/'posh' deli meats section) or more specialist food shops. The US brand **Vermont Creamery** has an award winning French-Style Crème Fraîche, although it is much creamier than the usual varieties you buy in the UK. Another similar product that can be used as a substitute is **Crema Mexicana**. This is widely available in US supermarkets, but you will sometimes need to look in the fridge section with Hispanic foods.
- **Fromage Frais** – virtually impossible to source in supermarkets in the USA, however, **Vermont Creamery** make **Fromage Blanc**, (the same thing as fromage frais) but I have yet to see it in any mainstream grocery stores.
- **Quark** – again, absent from most supermarkets in the US.
- A website called www.murrayscheese.com sells many varieties of European and specialist cheeses, including some of the items above.

6 – MEAT & FISH

America has one of the highest rates of meat consumption per capita in the world (second only to Luxembourg of all places). In fact, the average American consumes approximately 125kg of meat per year, which is equivalent to eating a 12oz steak every day! So, unsurprisingly, meat is very easy to purchase and is much cheaper than in the UK. This is particularly the case with poultry, beef and pork.

While we Brits tend to have a far more modest consumption of meat products, there is nothing quite as quintessentially British as a Sunday roast joint with all the trimmings. However, here in the US you will get very suspicious looks if you ask the butcher for a joint as this word does not have the same meaning for Americans … you're more likely to get referred to Narcotics Anonymous than be given a nice leg o' lamb!

Beef
The USDA (United States Department of Agriculture) grades all beef sold in supermarkets – the grades are Prime, Choice and Select. Prime is the best and has the most fat-

marbling making it more tender and flavourful, but less than 3% of beef in supermarkets is this grade and it is usually expensive. USDA Choice is high quality and is often leaner than Prime (due to less fat marbling). USDA Select is the leanest of beef sold in retail markets and it has an acceptable quality, but is much less tender and juicy than more expensive grades.

If you're being pedantic you could argue that all fresh meat qualifies as 'natural', however, meat products labelled 'natural' cannot contain any artificial flavour or flavouring, colouring ingredient, chemical preservative, or any other artificial or synthetic ingredient; and the product and its ingredients are not more than minimally processed. This means that most beef can be classified as 'natural' even if the cattle were exposed to antibiotics, synthetic growth hormones and/or raised in a 'feedlot' (75% of the beef sold in the supermarkets comes from cattle that are fed grains in a feedlot, or pen, rather than allowed to graze pasture). If these are things you are concerned about, it is important to check the packaging as the company is required to provide a statement that explains what they mean by the term "natural".

Another thing to note, particularly regarding minced beef products is that they will often have multiple countries of origin listed – a slightly confusing and alarming prospect. The 'mixing' of meats from different sources is actually often intentional. They blend leaner beef from Australia and New Zealand (where the cattle is usually grass fed on pastures) with the fattier beef from other places (where cattle are grain fed in feedlots)... this is how they can specify that a pack of meat is 85% lean or 96% lean... it's all in the mix! It can also reflect animals that are born in one place, but then moved and reared and processed elsewhere. The only way to ensure that your minced meat products are 'unmixed' is to choose a piece of sirloin or topside from the meat counter and ask the butcher to mince it for you. Personally, I wouldn't stress too much!

The biggest difference as a consumer is in the cuts of meat available. As mentioned already, the term 'joint' is never applied to meat in the US! Compare the two diagrams below to see the slight difference in nomenclature between the US & UK for cuts of beef.

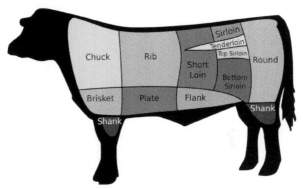

Figure 3: USA Beef cuts

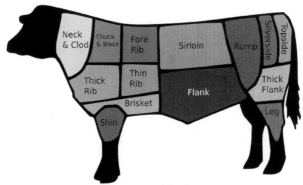

Figure 4: British Beef cuts

The important differences to remember are summarised below:

- **Ground beef** = Minced beef
- **Round beef for roasting** = Topside or silverside roasting joint
- **Tenderloin steak** = Fillet steak
- **Porterhouse steak** = Sirloin steak (UK)
- **Sirloin steak (US)** = Rump steak
- **Flank steak** = Beef skirt
- **Salt beef** = Corned beef

Pork

Fresh Pork

Pork is another very popular meat in the US. Unlike beef, pork isn't graded in the same way and so all the fresh pork sold in the supermarket is graded at 'acceptable', whereas, lower quality meats are graded 'utility' and are then used in processed products only. Again, you need to bear in mind that the label 'natural' only means that the meat has had no artificial flavours, colours, or preservatives added and has been minimally processed (i.e. minced). You will need to examine the packaging in greater detail to get more information about the way the animal was reared (e.g. hormone or antibiotic use, and conditions).

The cuts of meat are differently named, and can cause some confusion. When relatively new to the US, I went looking in the supermarket for a nice roasting 'joint' (see my explanation in the previous section about the use of this term), and was pretty dismayed to find a large cut of pork labelled a 'Boston Butt'. While I am a confirmed carnivore and more than happy to enjoy a leg of pork with crackling, apple sauce and all the trimmings, I felt that describing the poor piggy's rear end in such a crude way was a bit unnecessary! As it turned out, a Butt is from the shoulder ... in fact, in the UK it is the joint known as a pork hand. The reason it is called a Butt is historical, and refers to the way that these cuts of meat were stored in barrels (known as "butts") for storage and shipment.

A leg of pork for roasting is quite uncommon in America, where most leg cuts are used for ham. You may have to order in advance from your supermarket butcher or even go to a specialist butcher to get a proper leg of skin-on pork for the traditional roast with crackling.

Compare the two diagrams below for the differences in cuts between the USA & UK:

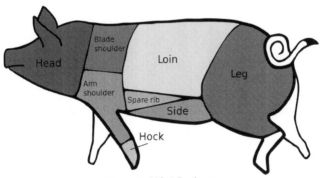

Figure 5: USA Pork cuts

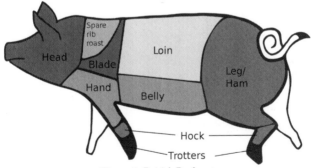

Figure 6: British Pork cuts

Pork loin steaks and cutlets (chops) are readily available and quite cheap, as are pork ribs... often sold in great big slabs for marinating and barbecuing or smoking!

Hams/Gammons

Gammon is a British word for a cured but uncooked hind leg of pork, and is a term that is not recognised or understood in the US. In the US all pork legs are known as ham, whether they have been cured or not. Even gammon steaks that that you'd serve with a pineapple ring are known as ham steaks. Hams are hugely popular in America, particularly for holidays such as Christmas, but there are so many different types that it can be confusing. For that reason, it is always really important to read the label carefully. Hams can be categorised as follows:

- **Fresh ham** – this is a ham that has not been cured (salted or smoked) or cooked, and it will always have the term "fresh" on the label. They require full cooking before eating, and you can partly boil, then glaze and roast them, as you would for a gammon joint.

- **Pre-cooked ham** – most hams you buy in supermarkets have been pre-cooked... you could literally eat them cold from the package. However, most people like to finish them off before serving, and this usually involves glazing them and studding with cloves and then reheating. Check the packaging carefully for added water, as sometimes the ham may have had up to 35% water added and thus best avoided!

- **Country ham** – sometimes known as a Virginia, Tennessee or Kentucky ham, these are dry cured (with a salt rub) and then smoked and aged. They usually need soaking before cooking because of the salt rub, but will still taste saltier than a fresh ham.

- **Picnic ham** – this is technically a pre-cooked ham, however, because of its extra fat it really benefits from additional cooking to taste its best!

Some British friends of ours here in Houston are big fans of roasted gammon and they spent a long time trying different brands and types to find one that was close to those they were used to buying and cooking in the UK. In their experience, many hams are hickory smoked and they found this not to their taste. After a fair bit of trial and error, they have found one they like and recommend, **Smithfield Hardwood Smoked Ham.**

Bacon

Sigh. Oh, how I miss you, 'proper' Bacon. Here in the US, bacon is almost always the streaky variety cut from belly pork, and you will get blank looks of confusion if you ask for sliced back bacon. In some International supermarkets, you may be lucky to get back bacon, but it certainly isn't the norm. If you're lucky it will be located in the 'International' freezer section, rather than with the fresh bacon in the fridges. As a less popular product, it is usually stocked as a frozen item with a longer shelf life! **Tommy Moloney's Irish Back Bacon** is the brand usually available in places that stock frozen bacon and it's good! The bacon comes from free-range pigs reared on an Amish farm in Pennsylvania, but is cured with traditional techniques brought to America from Ireland by the Moloney family.

If, however, you can't live without your bacon sarnies and you are struggling to find a local stockist... never fear as there is a solution! You can order British style meat products, including back bacon from a number of online suppliers. You will of course have to pay a hefty price for these compared to what you'd pay in the supermarket, but it may just be worth it!

- www.tommymoloneys.com - as described above, Tommy Moloney's Irish back bacon is good! And if you cannot find it in your local international supermarket, you can order online! They also sell other meat products such as gammons, corned beef and sausages. The shipping costs are high as you'd expect, but you can buy in bulk and it doesn't work out much more than you'd pay in the supermarket. This can be particularly good if there are a number of you expats willing to share an order (and split the shipping costs)!

- www.balsonbutchers.com - A family business owned by Mike Balson (a British expat living in the US) and continuing his family's 500 year history in the butchery industry. His parent's run the famous RJ Balson & Sons Butcher's shop in Bridport, Dorset (which has been open in the same location since 1880). With such a good pedigree you can be sure to get your traditional rashers from them, although their range of products is limited to bacon and bangers!
- www.britishbacon.com - William's Pork stock Wiltshire-cure bacon as well as a number of other British pork-based products such as sausages, sausage rolls and pork pies.

As a somewhat inferior alternative to proper back bacon, you can try Canadian bacon. In Canada the preferred bacon is the back bacon we Brits are used to; however, the American version of "Canadian Bacon" is a bit variable. It is usually a processed slice of ham that resembles the ovoid part of a back bacon rasher, without the streaky thin 'tail' piece. While it tastes okay and is certainly less fatty than the streaky alternative, it isn't a match to proper back bacon (at least in my humble opinion).

Sausages

The majority of 'sausages' sold in America are the pre-cooked frankfurter or hot dog variety. The raw pork or beef sausages we are used to in Britain are available, but are commonly called breakfast sausages or breakfast links.

The term 'link' describes a sausage in a casing, rather than a patty or sold by the pound (as we would buy sausage meat). Breakfast links are often quite skinny, a bit like a long chipolata sausage. A popular brand of sausage links and sausage meat is **Jimmy Dean**.

In addition to the skinny plain pork breakfast links, you can buy different varieties of uncooked sausage links, seasoned with various herbs and spices; popular ones include Bratwurst, Sweet Italian (a mild sausage seasoned with fennel and/or aniseed), Hot Italian (same as the sweet but with the addition of red pepper flakes) and Chorizo (a red coloured raw pork sausage flavoured with dried smoked red peppers and not the same as the smoked and dry cured sausage more common in Europe).

For those who miss the traditional UK bangers, you can sometimes get lucky by looking in the freezer section of international supermarkets (as with the bacon described above). Lincolnshire sausages are a rare delicacy that I snap up if I see them!

Deli meats

Most supermarkets have a Delicatessen where you can purchase luncheon meats, sliced meats and hams. These are known collectively as 'cold cuts' in America. You can also buy popular pre-sliced cold cuts (such as ham and salami) in vacuum packs in the fridge section next to the processed cheeses. Some of these vary greatly in quality and they often contain a lot of water and preservatives. **Applegate Farms** and **Hormel Natural Choice** offer a nice range of sliced deli hams & sandwich meats that contain no preservatives and no artificial colours or flavours. **Boar's Head** is another popular premium brand available in both pre-sliced packages or on the deli counter. The selection of 'cold cuts' on the deli counter in the supermarket is generally good and comparable to what you would find in a UK deli, but some of the European names have slight differences:

- **Summer sausage** – this is any sausage that can be kept without refrigeration, but it's usually a mix of pork and another meat such as beef or venison; it is similar to the Spanish '**salchichón**'.
- **Bologna** – a popular sliced sausage made from very finely ground pork; somewhat similar to the Italian '**mortadella**'.
- **Head cheese** – a terrine made from the head of a calf or pig and often set in aspic jelly; known as '**brawn**' in England.
- **Liverwurst** – a pork liver spreadable **pâté**.

The thing I miss most from the UK (out of all the things described in this book) is a proper **Melton Mowbray pork pie**. I made the mistake of buying some VERY expensive American ones in British Specialty store here in Houston and regretted it very quickly. When I saw **Cameron's Pork Pies** emblazoned with the Union Jack in the freezer of the British Isles store in Houston, I thought I had hit the jackpot. I was very disappointed as they are nothing like the pork pies in the UK. However, whilst I haven't tried them, the **English Pork Pie Company** based in Vermont gets very good reviews and does a range of popular British items such as Melton Mowbray pork pies, Cornish pasties, steak & ale pies, bacon, black pudding, and others. Set up in 2007 by an English couple, you'd hope they know what a decent pork pie should be like!

- www.englishporkpiecompany.com

Scotch eggs are also not a popular delicatessen item, but thankfully, these are easy to make yourself. If you've never tried, don't be scared and check out Delia Smith's recipe… yum!

Poultry

Chicken and turkey are very popular and cheap meats in America. All store bought poultry is USDA inspected for wholesomeness, but grading for quality is voluntary. That being said, most poultry products available at a retail level will be grade A and so will be of good quality. No hormones are used in the raising of chickens or turkeys, and when antibiotics are used there is a mandatory 'withdrawal' period prior to slaughter to prevent residues in the bird. Birds reared without use of antibiotics are clearly labeled.

Something to look out for is poultry labeled "basted" or "self-basted". This means that the meat has been injected with a solution of butter, fat, stock, broth or water with seasoning/flavor enhancers (up to 3% by volume for bone-in poultry, and 8% for boneless). The label must identify this, including the % and ingredients.

Another thing to be aware of is the label "air-chilled". In the USA, the most common way to quickly chill the bird after slaughter is to dunk it in a tank of chlorinated iced water. In Europe, this practice is not allowed because of fears of food safety and birds are cooled individually using cold air instead. Another side effect of water cooling is that the bird meat absorbs some of the water, so some people prefer the taste of air chilled poultry which retains its natural juices. The availability of air-chilled poultry is becoming wider-spread in the US, particularly in the organic/natural foods market.

A small percentage of poultry sold in the USA undergoes a process whereby the meat is irradiated to control certain common bacteria on raw poultry that can cause illness when poultry is undercooked or otherwise mishandled. Packages of irradiated poultry are easily recognizable at the store because they must carry the "Radura" international radiation logo as well as the words "Treated with Irradiation" or "Treated by Irradiation." Whilst this

43

process has been given official endorsement by the American Medical Association, World Health Organisation and certified as safe by the US FDA (Food and Drug Administration) and been used in many countries for the last 50 years, it's still not very popular due to consumer concerns about safety and food quality. Something to note, is that meat labelled organic is not allowed to be irradiated.

Figure 6: The Radura symbol used by the US FDA to show a food has been treated with ionizing radiation.

Finally, there are a few differences to note in terms of names for things:

- **Variety meats** = Giblets/offal (e.g. kidney, liver, etc...)
- **Tender** = any strip of breast meat
- **Buffalo wing** = a chicken wing, popularized in the Buffalo district of New York where it is served with a cayenne pepper hot sauce.

Wot no Lamb?

Annual consumption of lamb (and mutton) in the US is very low – 0.36kg per person, compared to 25.6kg in New Zealand! However, as a multicultural nation, many recent immigrants to the U.S. originate from regions of the world where lamb (and goat) are commonly consumed. Consequently, there is a growing demand for lamb in the U.S., especially among people of specific ethnic backgrounds. As a consequence, buying lamb in most big chain supermarkets can be difficult with varying quality and variety of cuts available. It is easier to obtain good quality lamb from international and specialty supermarkets or try Halal butchers; for example there is a brilliant Deli and supermarket called Phoenicia in Houston that is a great place to buy good quality lamb.

Lamb in the USA is subject to the same USDA inspections for wholesomeness as other meat, but does not have to be graded for quality. The voluntary grading system is similar as for beef: Prime, Choice & Good. Both hormones and antibiotics are approved by the USDA for use in rearing lambs for meat and you can only be sure they haven't been used if they are clearly labeled as such. Lamb is often labeled 'natural' – as mentioned before, it's worth noting that all fresh meat qualifies as 'natural' regardless of the efforts of various brands to appeal to health-conscious consumers. However, if a product is labeled 'natural' it cannot contain any artificial flavor, flavouring, colouring, and chemical preservative or any other synthetic ingredient. Furthermore, it must be only minimally processed.

Cuts of lamb in the USA are similar to the UK, except that as with pork, lamb chops are known as lamb cutlets.

Fishy business

Fish is a popular dish in the US even if it's not synonymous with batter & chips as it is to us Brits! However, unlike the strict guidelines and regulations controlling the sale of meat, the fish & seafood industry is much less rigorously regulated. This doesn't mean that the fish available in the US is of an inferior quality just that the labelling of fish & seafood is a bit hit-or-miss; the USDA developed mandatory country-of-origin labelling rules in 2005, but there is no real enforcement of these. Furthermore, wholesale fish sellers and processed seafood is exempt. Because of these ineffective federal laws, some states (such as Alaska, Washington, Arkansas & Louisiana) have their own additional labelling regulations. There are a number of voluntary regulatory organisations that fisheries can associate themselves with, the most notable of which is the Marine Stewardship Council (MSC). MSC-certified fisheries adhere to sustainable practises and conform to strict traceability guidelines. Other certification programs exist, including Friend of the Sea, Global Trust Certifications Ltd, International Fishmeal & Fish Oil Organization (IFFO), Aquaculture Stewardship Council (ASC) and Best Aquaculture Practices. Look for the accompanying logo.

Figure 8: Various logos of seafood industry certification schemes

When buying fish in America it can be a little hard to make yourself understood, purely because of the difference in pronunciation. This is especially worth bearing in mind when trying to purchase a fillet of tuna, as you will get blank looks unless you ask for a "fillay of toona"!

Many fish in the supermarkets will be common to a British shopper such as salmon, cod, trout, tuna and halibut. However, there are a number of popular types of fish that are unfamiliar to people in the UK.

- **Catfish** – a very popular freshwater fish from the southern states, especially popular in Mississippi. It has firm, white flesh which has a 'meatier' texture than most other white fish. Its flavour is delicate and sweet.
- **Chilean Sea Bass** – a rich and moderately oily fish. It is tender and falls into large moist flakes. When cooked, the meat stays white and looks similar to cod. It's an easy fish to eat whole because of its bone structure.
- **Mahi mahi** – a Hawaiian favourite. It has a sweet taste similar to swordfish. The meat is lean and fairly firm (although not steak-like).
- **Red Snapper** – a lean, moist fish with a sweet, mild but distinctive flavour. It's considered one of the tastiest fish in the world so is quite expensive but good for a treat!
- **Tilapia** – a mild and sweet tasting freshwater fish with a firm and flaky texture. Tilapia is a very common white fish and is usually very good value.
- **Pollock** – this is the American name for coley or coalfish.

Sadly, mackerel is not a very common fish in the US, but you can occasionally find it tinned or smoked in more upmarket or international supermarkets.

Get yer fingers off my Fish sticks...
A fish finger sandwich on white bread with a squirt of tomato ketchup is the stuff dreams are made of! At least they are if you're an expat Brit living in America! Fish

fingers aren't exactly considered a delicacy (they are a cheap, processed food after all), but they are a beloved favourite of us Brits, and a staple nursery food for little ones. In Britain, the quality of the humble fish finger has dramatically increased since my own childhood, with premium brands making them from 100% fish fillet and 'natural' breadcrumbs, free from artificial nasties. You can even get 'pink' ones made with omega-3 rich salmon... posh, eh?!

In America, the nearest equivalent to a fish finger is called a 'fish stick' and the quality is variable with most brands using minced white fish of unknown variety (plus some filler). They are often battered rather than breaded too! Since moving to Texas, I have tended to make my own 'fish fingers' from fresh fillets of fish and then freeze them for use later (a recipe for these can be found on my blog www.mamawithideas.com/2012/04/brain-boosting-fish-fingers-for-kids.html). It's surprisingly easy, tasty and economical! However, for convenience sake, a brand that makes high quality frozen breaded fish sticks from whole fish fillets without any artificial additives is **Dr Praeger's Sensible Foods**. If not located in the mainstream frozen fish section of your supermarket, look in the 'natural' or imported frozen foods section.

Smoked fish
Smoked fish is easy to find in the refrigerator next to the fresh fish counter in most supermarkets. Smoked salmon is available, although it is often easier to get **Lox**. Although cured in brine, lox is *not* smoked whereas traditional Scottish smoked salmon is brined and then cold smoked. In reality, the word lox is used for both brined & cold smoked salmon in the US and the taste difference is subtle and unnoticeable unless you are a connoisseur. While discussing smoked salmon, I will mention that the Russian **cocktail blinis** that are quite popular in the UK for creating appetizers are very difficult to locate in the

supermarkets. Again you will have to search for them in the more specialist delis. I found that they were quite easy to make yourself (a simple buckwheat flour batter and the same method as for drop scones) and can be made and frozen ahead of time!

As mentioned already, it is possible to find smoked mackerel, but it's quite unusual and you may need to look in upscale supermarkets or specialist delis. Finally, if you're after kippers for your breakfast, you will need to ask for smoked herring! It is usually only available in cans, for example, you can buy **John West Kipper Fillets in Oil** in the international aisle of some supermarkets. Unfortunately, whole split smoked kippers aren't hugely popular so you may struggle to find them in your local supermarket. As for smoked mackerel, you may need to look in more specialist delicatessens or order online. Try **Robert Wholey & Co.**:

- www.wholey.com/smokedfish.html.

Shellfish (excluding shrimp)
Shellfish, and in particular lobster, is very popular in the US. Most large supermarkets have a live tank in the fish department where you can choose your own lobster (in some places you can buy fish live too). There is usually a wide selection of clams, crabs, mussels, oysters, lobsters, crayfish (or crawfish) and scallops on the fresh fish counter or in the freezer section.

Shrimp or Prawns
The whole shrimp vs. prawn thing is very confusing as it's not clear what the definitions of each are! Some countries say the shrimp is bigger; some countries say that the prawn is bigger. Some countries define prawns as freshwater species and shrimp as marine, while in other countries the opposite is true. Some even say that they're all named shrimp; some say they're all named prawn. Personally, I'd

rather keep out of this one and leave it up to the biologists and culinary experts!

However, for the purpose of this book I will simply say that what we would call prawns in the UK are called shrimp here in the US. So, in a restaurant you would get a shrimp cocktail for an appetiser, rather than a prawn cocktail!

Usually fresh shrimp are sold whole and uncooked, but you can buy frozen (in fact this is probably better if you don't live near a coastal area as shrimp does not store well and should ideally be eaten within 24 hours). Shrimp is sold **by count** rather than by than a description of the size. The count represents the number of shrimp in a pound for a given size category, for example, "Jumbo" shrimp have a count of 21/25 (with an average of 23 shrimps per pound) whereas, "Small" shrimp have a count of 51/60 (with an average of 55 shrimps per pound).

7 – CANNED GOODS, COOKING SAUCES & MEAL HELPERS

Canned (or tinned) food is as popular in the US as it is the UK with a wide variety of foods available in cans. The range of canned vegetables is similar to the UK with tomatoes, sweet corn, peas etc… dominating the shelves. Canned meat is also widely available, with products like **Spam** and **salt beef (corned beef)** and corn beef hash easy to find.

Canned Fish

Canned (tinned) tuna is as popular in the US as the UK with brands like **Starkist** dominating the market, but there are a few differences in the labelling you will need to get your head around. You will see tuna described as **chunk light** or **Albacore solid white**. Chunk light tuna is simply tuna that isn't white and is primarily made up from a species called skipjack, but it can include others such as yellowfin and tongol or combinations of different species. The 'light' adjective is used as it is usually slightly lower in fat & calories, but this is misleading as it is actually lower in the good omega-3 essential fatty acid. The 'chunk' refers to the fact that the tuna in the can will be in pieces of varying size and texture. In the UK, most canned tuna is chunk light.

In contrast, solid white tuna must come from the Albacore species, and is canned in 'solid' steak-like pieces. The flesh is pale cream rather than the pink we Brits are used to. It is considered to be of better quality, with a milder taste and higher levels of omega-3 than cheaper chunk light tuna. However, it has also been shown to have higher levels of mercury than chunk light. One last thing to note is that Albacore tuna is nearly always line-caught and so is more dolphin-friendly.

Canned **sardines** have declined in popularity in the US with the last large US sardine cannery closing in 2010. Therefore, canned sardines are mostly imported. You may find them near the canned tuna or you may see **John West's** canned sardines in the International aisle.

Every type of beans except Heinz

Beans of every variety are available in cans from adzuki to black to cannellini. Plain beans in salt water are referred to as recipe beans and a popular brand is **Bush's Best**. Beans in sauces are also very popular with every type of 'baked beans' that you could imagine, including the infamous Boston Beans (flavoured with molasses and pork), honey baked beans, maple cured bacon beans and barbeque beans to name but a few.

Beans with a Tex-Mex slant are also hugely popular with refried beans, and varieties of frijoles & pintos featuring prominently. **Old El Paso** is a brand that many Brits will be familiar with.

For familiar baked beans that you will recognise, the best thing is to head to the International aisle for **Heinz** or **Branston Baked Beans**. You can also buy them online.

Ready-made soup

Campbell's soups are very popular, often with large dominating display racks of their own in the soup aisle. They have a full range of the familiar condensed soups, but many contain High Fructose Corn Syrup (HFCS). In response to consumer demand, Campbell's have brought out a range called **Campbell's 100% natural** that contain no artificial ingredients, flavourings, colourings or preservatives.

British favourites such as **Heinz Cream of Tomato soup** can be found in the International aisle of most supermarkets but are expensive. **Pacific Foods** do large cartons of Organic Creamy Tomato soup (plus a low sodium variety) that are a good substitute for Heinz.

Cooking sauces

Pasta sauces are very popular and there are a wide range of marinara, ragù and carbonara sauces available in jars. Popular brands include **Ragú** (manufactured by Unilever, but a sister brand of the Ragú manufactured by Knorr in the UK) who have organic and light sauces in addition to their usual varieties. Another brand with increasing popularity is **Prego** (manufactured by the Campbell Soup Company) that has a wide variety of flavours and often costs less than its competition.

Meal helpers

Meal Helpers are essentially boxed kits for dinners that you can cook in one-pan. They usually contain dried pasta with a packet of sauce mix or seasoning and the cook simply adds water or milk (plus cooked meat, fish and/or veg as optional extras) to make up the meal. The term is based on the popular American brand '**Hamburger Helper**' that has been around since 1971, but is now applied to all pre-prepared meals of this kind and there is usually an aisle in the supermarket dedicated to meals of this kind. The most common type of these is a variant on

the ever-popular American classic macaroni & cheese...
Kraft Mac 'n' Cheese is the most popular brand. An
increasingly popular organic version is made by **Annie's
Homegrown**.

8 CHAPTER NAME

Bread

The difference in bread is one thing that takes getting used to when anywhere abroad, not least in America. We Brits are used to high quality processed sliced breads, whether soft, white and fluffy (and perfect for a bacon butty) or brown, wholesome and grainy (and the perfect abutment to grated cheddar & pickle). So, it comes as quite a shock when the sliced sandwich breads available in the supermarket taste so ... wrong. Too sweet? Full of high fructose corn syrup? Too dense and squishy and ... moist? Finding the right adjective to explain why the vast majority of sliced breads available in the supermarkets don't suit the British palate is hard. But there is no escaping the fact that a lack of decent sliced sandwich bread is the lament of many British expats.

When we first moved to the US I quickly resorted to buying a bread machine in an attempt to recreate the taste and texture of bread that my family would eat, but the daily grind of having to bake bread (even if a lot of the grunt work is taken out of the equation by the machine) soon became a chore. So, I went on a long (and at times painful) search for decent replacement bread.

First off, skip the supermarket aisle full of packaged sandwich bread. I went through countless brands and varieties of bread and was continually disappointed. Instead, head for the artisan bread section (or bakery) near the produce section. Here, you will find breads baked on site and the quality is far superior. Secondly, unless you know what it tastes like and actually like the taste, I wouldn't recommend the very popular sourdough even though it looks delicious. It's… well… sour. In most artisan bread departments you will find decent whole wheat, oat and multigrain loaves that compare well to the varieties in the UK. French style bread (but in loaves not baguettes) is also popular. It is finding decent white bread that often poses the problem; and this is often a double problem for people with small fussy children who can smell non-Kingsmill bread a mile off! Ask for English Toasting bread and you will get a decent 'familiar' if quite small loaf. It is somewhat drier than I would like but as the name suggests is great for toast! Another good bet is to look for Homestyle White Bread. This has become our go to white bread for sandwiches. Most of the loaves of bread in the Artisan bread section will be unsliced, but you can ask the staff in the bakery to slice and re-wrap it for you.

Breakfast Cereal

For many families, a favourite breakfast cereal is the staple of a child's diet (and some adults too)! My kids in particular have definite preferences for certain brands and types of cereal, and it was even worse when we first moved to the US and our 17 month old twins were in a very picky phase. Luckily, many of the UK favourites are available in the US, although it may take a while to pick them out of the line-up of sugary, colourful, marshmallow-laden, chocolaty types on offer! I have picked out the top selling UK breakfast cereals and listed them with relevant information and/or equivalents:

- All of the Kellogg's cereals we know and love are available in the US, even if they have slightly different names and packaging, because Kellogg's is actually an American company. **Cornflakes, Crunchy Nut Cornflakes, All Bran, Bran Flakes, Special K, Shredded Wheat** and **Rice Krispies** are all available and very popular. **Frosties** are called **Kellogg's Frosted Flakes** (just look for Tony the Tiger!) and **Coco Pops** are called **Cocoa Krispies**, but both are also very popular.

- **Cheerios** (produced by General Mills in the US rather than Nestlé) are also very popular. There are lots of different varieties available, but it's worth noting that the 'standard' Cheerios are different in the UK to the US. In the US, Original Cheerios are a plain oat variety (in a yellow box) and they are much less sweet than the ones we have in the UK. In the UK, the Original Cheerios are multi-grain. Multi-Grain Cheerios are available in the US, but they are considered one of the 'variations' on the standard. The packaging is a purple and white box.

- **Shreddies** are sadly not available in the US. However, there are a number of brands that have similar equivalents. **Cascadian Farms Multigrain Squares** are a good alternative and my kids have made the switch fairly easily. Chex is also a popular brand that gets its name from the checkerboard square shape of the cereal. **Wheat Chex** are similar to Shreddies.

- **Weetabix** is available in the US (thank goodness, otherwise our stay in America would have been brief). It is sometimes found in the International aisle with other British imports, but is increasingly found in the normal cereal section. The packaging & logo is the same as the UK (in spite of being manufactured in the US) so it should be quite distinctive; however, as it's not a very popular brand it is often either on the very top shelf or the very bottom so do look carefully! **Alpen Muesli** (another Weetabix product) is also available.

- Porridge is called oatmeal in the US and is a popular breakfast cereal. **Quaker Oats** are easily found, but the popular on-the-go variety from the UK, **Oat So Simple**, is not. Instead, Quaker sell **Instant Oatmeal**; a similar product. Unfortunately, **Ready Brek** is not available and there isn't a straightforward alternative. A popular product made from wheat rather than oats is called **Cream of Wheat** (and is essentially farina or semolina). **Grits** is also a popular hot cereal derived from ground corn rather than oats.

Pasta and rice

Not a lot to say about pasta and rice, as the range of varieties is similar to that available in the UK. One thing to note is that pasta made with eggs is referred to as noodles, so you may see lasagne noodles, whereas we Brits think of noodles as exclusively associated with Asian cuisine. Alternatively, pasta made without eggs and thickened with durum wheat is called macaroni regardless of the shape! Capisce? Me neither!

Other slight variations are in the names of things. For example, in the US vermicelli pasta is thinner than spaghetti, whereas in Europe it is thicker. Call me heathen, but pasta is pasta and the differences are trivial!

Fresh pasta is often available in the deli fridge section, with a selection of stuffed tortellini and ravioli types. A popular brand is **Buitoni**.

Rice is a common agricultural product in the US and about 85% of the rice sold in the supermarkets was actually grown in America. Varieties include short-, medium-, and long-grain rice, as well as organic and specialty rice such as jasmine, basmati and Arborio.

Flours

There are a multitude of flours available in the grocery stores, milled from all kinds of grains, seeds and nuts. However, the most common one is called **All Purpose Flour**. This is the same as **plain** white wheat flour in the UK. You can buy it **bleached** or **unbleached** and **bromated** or **un-bromated** (see chapter 3 for more on this). As in the UK, quality varies and so it's worth spending the extra on premium brands. Popular brands include **Gold Medal** and **King Arthur Flour**.

Self-Raising flour is not very popular outside of the southern states of America. Known in America as **Self-Rising flour**, it is increasingly available, but still not that common. It is very easy to replicate though: simply add 1-and-a-half teaspoons of baking powder and a pinch of salt for every US cup (125g) of all-purpose flour required in your recipe.

Whole wheat flours are common and can be used in place of **Graham Flours** when required in an American recipe (coarse grained, whole wheat Graham flours are named after a Presbyterian minister from the 19th century who espoused on the benefits of whole grains). Graham flours are still available in some supermarkets and whole foods stores, but are rarely used in things like Graham crackers which get their name from the flour!

For coarse grained flours made from other grains/seeds, the word 'meal' is often used. So for example, almond flour (or **ground almonds**) is known as **almond meal**. For more unusual flours and meals, **Bob's Red Mill** has a brilliant range. If not immediately obvious, this brand is sometimes located in the 'natural foods' section of mainstream supermarkets.

Cornflour is a slightly confusing one. We Brits think of cornflour as a fine, white starchy powder that is used as a thickening agent in stocks & gravies. In the US, cornflour is literally yellow flour made from ground corn kernels and used in things like cornbread. This is often also called **corn meal** in the US. To get the white thickening agent, you will need to look for **corn starch**. **Kingsford's** is a popular brand that comes in a square plastic yellow tub with a blue lid.

Sugar & syrup

The standard sugar sold in the US is called **granulated cane sugar** and is the same as white granulated sugar in the UK. It is sometimes a more natural light golden colour instead of white, but don't be fooled into thinking it's better for you, it just means it has a higher molasses content. Many Brits struggle looking for **caster sugar** for their baking. Caster sugar is the same as normal cane sugar except that it is finer grained (the grains are small enough to pass through a sugar sprinkler or 'caster'). In the US, you simply need to look for cane sugar labelled 'superfine'. It is also sometimes called **Baker's sugar** or **Bar sugar**. In a pinch, you can simply put normal cane sugar in your food processor and run it for a minute or so. This will make the texture much finer, similar to caster sugar.

There are a number of **brown sugars** available such as light brown, dark brown, and muscovado. **Demerara sugar** is not very popular in the US, but is sometimes available and labelled **'raw' sugar**. Another popular type of 'raw' sugar similar to Demerara is **Turbinado sugar**. It differs slightly in texture (being slightly coarser grained) and taste (more honey-like than molasses), but is a good substitute for use in teas and coffees.

Icing sugar is known as **Confectioner's** or **Powdered sugar** in the US. In actual fact, it is slightly less fine than real icing sugar but works just as well. Nearly all brands add a small amount of corn starch, maltodextrin or tricalcium phosphate to the confectioner's sugar to stop it from hardening, however, with better brands this is a smaller percentage. **King Arthur Flour** carry a product called **Glazing Sugar** which is a good, high quality and very fine icing sugar.

Treacle and **golden syrup** are not common in the US. **Molasses** (sometimes called **blackstrap**) is very popular in the US and is very similar to dark treacle and can be substituted. Sadly, there isn't an American equivalent to Golden syrup; however, imported **Tate & Lyle Golden syrup** (and T&L treacle) is sometimes available (usually in the International section of the supermarket).

Fats

Canola oil is the most common vegetable oil available in the US, but we Brits know it as **Rapeseed oil**. It is no different in taste to standard vegetable oil available in the UK. It is low in saturated fat and contains both omega-6 and omega-3 fatty acids, so is considered quite a healthy oil as they go. There are a wide variety of other seed & nut oils available in the supermarkets. **Olive Oil** is also very popular and you can get a range of excellent quality extra virgin olive oils.

For **suet**, you will need to ask at a specialist butcher (or you might get lucky at the butcher's counter in the supermarket) and you'll get a large block of fresh pork fat suet which you can shred at home… obviously this is not the vegetarian stuff! For dehydrated & vegetarian shredded suet, you will need to look for the familiar **Atora** brand in the International aisle of your supermarket.

Lard as we Brits know it is hard to come by. However, **Manteca** is the Spanish word for lard and it's quite popular in Hispanic cooking. Most supermarkets in the US have a Hispanic section and you can find Manteca there. It is often not in the fridge section which is strange to us Brits, but that is because it has been hydrogenated to help it stay solid at room temperature and have a longer shelf life. Hydrogenated fats are not as bad as partially hydrogenated fats (trans fats), but it's not as if you didn't know that lard isn't something you should eat to excess anyway!

Vegetable Shortening (a solid block of vegetable fat) is very popular in the US and is frequently used as an alternative to lard in baking. The most popular brand is **Crisco** (and is similar to the UK brand **Cookeen**). In my opinion, it has a much softer texture than lard and doesn't substitute well in pastry making. You may want to look for fully hydrogenated vegetable shortening to avoid the problematic trans fats, although it's worth remembering that according to the FDA, "Food manufacturers are allowed to list amounts of trans fat with less than 0.5 gram (1/2 g) per serving as 0 (zero) on the Nutrition Facts panel". **Earth Balance Natural Shortening** is a vegan and non-GMO version that can be found in the 'natural' foods fridge section.

Dried Herbs & spices
The selection of dried herbs & spices available in US grocery stores is vast. In the main, you can find the majority of familiar types that you would get in the UK. There are a few notable exceptions:

- **Mixed herbs** is a blend that is so common in the UK that I was totally confused when I couldn't find it here in the US! **Italian mixed herbs** is the closest you will get to the British dried mixed herbs blend. It has a slightly higher proportion of oregano to the other herbs but the difference is negligible in a recipe. I initially tried the **Provence**

herbs mix, but found the dried lavender really overpowering.

- **Mixed spice** is another one that I assumed was a commonly available thing, but again it proved to be a country specific blend. Don't be confused by the ground Allspice and assume this is a good substitute for Mixed Spice – this is the name of a spice, rather than a blend! In fact, ground allspice berries are one of the ingredients in mixed spice mix! In some specialty stores you may find it, but it will be called **Pudding Spice**. The closest thing available in the mainstream supermarkets is the very popular **Pumpkin pie spice mix** – it is similar enough that you can substitute it, but it doesn't contain any coriander so you may want to add a knife tip of dried coriander to your recipe. You can also make your own... 16 parts ground cinnamon, 8 parts ground coriander, 4 parts ground allspice, 2 parts ground ginger, 2 parts ground nutmeg and 1 part ground cloves.

- **Bouquet garni** is not available in the US. However, you can make your own: tie together with a string or wrap securely in cheesecloth: 4 sprigs fresh parsley or chervil, 1 sprig fresh thyme, and 1 bay leaf. Alternatively, you can substitute equal parts parsley, thyme, and crushed bay leaf *OR* equal parts chervil, thyme, and crushed bay leaf *OR* equal parts basil, marjoram, and summer savory.

- **Curry powder** is available in most supermarket spice aisles; however, I have been quite disappointed with the ones that I have tried. Indian food is not as popular in the US as it is in the UK, and so the variety and quality of Indian spices and foods available in the mainstream supermarkets is not often very good. **Patak's** curry pastes are sometimes available in the

International aisles and I've found these to be a more consistent solution to using curry powder. In larger cities, you may find that there is a district with a lot of southern Asian supermarkets and restaurants. Here in Houston, there are a number of Indian and southern Asian supermarkets around the Harwin and Hillcroft intersection ... in fact it is known locally as Little India. It is much easier to find decent curry spices and things like **garam masala** in these places than in the main grocery stores. Also try specialty or import supermarkets.

- **Aniseed** is known as **anise** in the US.
- **Stem ginger** – see more in the Christmas section in chapter 15.

Stocks & gravies

In America, **gravy** is not as clearly defined as we think of it, encompassing a wide range of sauces that are often thicker than gravy in the UK. Popular types include cream gravy (a thick, pale creamy sauce, often served with fried chicken), egg gravy (a sauce made by adding eggs and flour to bacon drippings and served with breakfast 'biscuits') and white gravy (a thick sauce made with meat drippings, flour and milk). To get ready-made gravy as we think of it, you need to ask for a **brown gravy mix**. These are usually in individual sachets that you mix with hot water to make up as needed. **McCormick** is a popular brand. For those used to gravy granules and powder, **Bisto** is commonly available in the International aisle of the supermarket but is usually expensive.

In the UK, most people prepare ready-made **stock** from dehydrated stock cubes such as those made by **Oxo** or **Knorr**. In the US, stock is usually sold in cartons or cans ready to use. There are a wide range of types but the most common are beef, chicken and vegetable. Low sodium varieties are also often available. If you prefer stock cubes, they are sometimes available but are often easily overlooked. Ask for **bouillon cubes** (pronounced BOOL-yon) and look in the Hispanic section if not in the aisle with the tinned stocks. The most common brand available is **Knorr**. Another good alternative is to ask for a food base. These are concentrated pastes that can be made into stocks with hot water. A popular one is **Better Than Bouillon** made by the **Superior Touch** brand. Better Than Bouillon also has vegetarian versions of 'beef' and 'chicken' stocks. And for Brits that can't do without their **Oxo cubes**, these are frequently stocked in the International aisle of the supermarket.

Tom-ay-do paste

Tomato puree in England is bought as a concentrated paste in a squeeze-y, toothpaste-like tube. In the US, **tomato puree** is essentially tinned tomatoes that have been pureed to a sauce-like consistency. In fact, it is most commonly sold in a tin although sometimes available in glass jars. To get the concentrated tomato puree in a tube, you need to ask for **concentrated tomato paste**. It will be usually located in the pasta aisle with the more expensive imported Italian pastas and pesto sauces and **Amore** is the usual brand seen. However, you may also find it in the International aisle of your supermarket if they have a 'Mediterranean' section. It is worth bearing this in mind when following American recipes, as they often call for larger quantities of tomato puree than you would imagine... this is because they don't mean the concentrated stuff!

9 – CONDIMENTS

Every world cuisine has its preferred condiments and the US is no different... thankfully some of them are shared with those us Brits favour. For those other sauces and accompaniments that are peculiar to our British palate, never fear as there are sources (excuse the homophonic pun) stateside!

Sauces

Interestingly, salsa is now more popular than ketchup in the US (thanks to the influence of the growing Hispanic communities); however, ketchup is still a hugely popular mealtime favourite. Heinz ketchup is the number 1 ketchup, but look for the **Simply Heinz Ketchup** variety if you are concerned about High Fructose Corn Syrup (HFCS). **Hunt's** is another nice brand of tomato ketchup.

Brown sauce is not really used in the States although the closest thing to it is called Steak sauce. For the real deal, you will need to look in the International aisle where you can usually find **HP** or **Daddies** brown sauce (and sometimes **HP Fruity**).

Mustard in the US is not what we Brits are used to. It is a very mild yellow condiment and is often used liberally (warn American friends that English Mustard is not the same before they slather it on a hot dog as one of my husband's colleagues did)! Other mustards such as **Dijon & wholegrain mustards** are also popular. Strong English Mustard like **Colman's** is not common and usually only available in the International aisle or online. You can sometimes find **Colman's Mustard Powder** there too.

Wine, cider, rice, balsamic and countless fruit flavoured vinegars are evident on the shelves, but brown malt vinegar is often difficult to spot in such a multitude as it's not as popular as in the UK. Look for Crosse & Blackwell, Heinz, and London Pub brands. Imported Sarson's is usually located in the International aisle.

At first you may struggle to see **Lea & Perrin's Worcestershire sauce** in the mainstream sections of the US supermarkets. Its packaging is slightly different with a beige label instead of orange and it comes wrapped in paper (although the font on the packaging is as distinctive as ever). On close inspection it's evident that the recipe is not quite the same: the biggest difference is that distilled white vinegar is used in place of malt vinegar. Regardless of the small differences the American version tastes almost identical to the British recipe. It used to be manufactured with High Fructose Corn Syrup (HFCS), but since 2011 the US version has reverted to using traditional sugar!

BBQ sauce - There are literally hundreds of varieties of BBQ sauce available and the choice is a little overwhelming. Popular varieties include: Texas BBQ Sauce (heavily seasoned & spicy sauce with only a touch of tomato and little or no sugar), Kansas City BBQ Sauce (a thick reddish-brown tomato based sauce with sugar, vinegar & spices) and South Carolina BBQ Sauce (a yellowish sauce made primarily of mustard, vinegar, sugar & spices).

Pickles

Pickled gherkins (known simply as 'pickles' in the US), **olives** and **sauerkraut** are very popular in the US and there is a wide selection available.

Other pickled vegetables such as **pickled onion, red cabbage** and **beetroot** are rarely seen in the mainstream section of the supermarket and so you will have to look in the international aisle. **Hayward's** is a popular imported brand.

Similarly with **piccalilli** or **chutney**, these are not popular condiments in the US so you will have to look in the international section. **Branston Pickle** is usually available, but also only in the international section.

Roast dinner accompaniments

In the US, the term **Horseradish sauce** refers to grated horseradish combined with mayonnaise and is popular and commonly available, although most American's use it as a sandwich condiment rather than with Roast Beef. To get the more traditional horseradish mixed with vinegar as we Brits are used to, you will have to look for '**Prepared Horseradish**'. To make an authentic British horseradish sauce, simply add sour cream (and some optional garlic) to prepared horseradish and mix.

Mint sauce is often only seen as a neon green jelly. For proper mint sauce you will probably have to look in the International aisle where you will usually find **Colman's** imported. Similarly, **Cranberry sauce** is often also 'jellied' so look for Whole Berry Cranberry sauce for a more traditional texture.

Bread sauce is not a common accompaniment but you can find the **Colman's** packet mixes in the International section too if you'd rather have the convenience of not making it yourself.

Stuffing mixes are common, but they are often much

coarser in texture than we Brits are accustomed to, with large cubes of bread. **Pepperidge Farm** has a variety of stuffing flavours including the traditional sage & onion. However, if you want to stick to the familiar then **Paxo** stuffing mixes are available in the International aisle.

Salad dressings

Mayonnaise is the most popular condiment in the US, outselling both ketchup and salsa! Popular brands include **Hellman's** and **Miracle Whip**.

There are many varieties of **salad dressings** available, the most popular being **Ranch**. Quality brands to consider are **Hidden Valley**, **Newman's Own** & **Annie's**. Some gourmet salad dressings are located in the fridges next to the salad in the Produce section.

Heinz salad cream is only available in international aisle or specialty online stores.

10 – DRINKS

Water

Tap water in the US is potable and classed as safe for consumption; however, many Americans choose to drink only bottled water as a 'healthier' option. Unfortunately, in 1993 there was a severe outbreak of cryptosporidium from contaminated tap water in Milwaukee, Wisconsin, which led to several deaths and around 400,000 illnesses that has somewhat clouded the issue. However, in spite of the bad press that high profile cases like these give to municipal water supply (there were several cases in the UK during the 1990's too) tap water in the US is safely drinkable for most healthy individuals. That being said, many people choose not to drink the tap water anyway as it does taste very chlorinated in some areas. The tap water is also fluoridated (as in the UK).

Unfortunately, your options aren't really that straightforward. An estimated 25% of bottled water sold in America is actually repackaged tap water that (as a low-risk food product) undergoes less testing than the rigorously monitored municipal tap water supply! Some may have undergone further filtering and others not;

unfortunately, they are not required to specify. Surprisingly, premium brands such as **Dasani** (manufactured by Coca-Cola Company) and **Aquafina** (produced by PepsiCo Inc.) are simply bottled municipal water. Even brands such as **Ozarka**, who market their main product as 100% Natural Spring Water, have ranges of bottled water from municipal supply. They have almost the same packaging, but are labelled 'distilled' or 'drinking' water. Check the labels carefully. The bottles themselves are also often manufactured from plastics with questionable safety issues, and there are also the obvious environmental concerns of using so much plastic!

A good alternative is to use a water filter. Common ones available in the US are made by **Brita** & **Pur** (both these brands are available in the UK too, so if you have a filter jug already you will easily be able to buy replacement filters in the US). These have activated carbon and ion exchange filters that act to remove some impurities and the taste and smell of chlorine.

Tea

This is often the thing that Brits abroad miss the most… a decent cuppa tea! Most Americans think of tea as a cold drink that is iced, without milk and often sweetened with honey, sugar or fruit. You can buy teabags in the supermarkets but they are frequently for herbal teas, rather than a traditional brew that you would add milk to. If you want tea as we think of it, you must ask for hot, black tea. **Lipton** is the most common brand and most American's use these teabags to make iced tea rather than drink it hot. However, it is (in my opinion) weak and has a weird bitter taste that reminds me of the scalding hot, cheap tea you get in a polystyrene cup from a dodgy burger van!

Twinings is available in most supermarkets although it is their **Earl Grey** tea that is most common (packaged in a pale yellow box). You can also sometimes find their

English Breakfast teabags (in a red box). Thankfully, you can also buy good ol' **PG Tips** or **Yorkshire Tea** bags in the International aisle of bigger grocery stores. Just be prepared to pay a lot of money for it! Ordering in bulk online is often a cheaper way of doing it, with online stores like Amazon offering discounts for subscribing to their products (you stipulate how many you want and how often you want it delivered).

If you're stuck for a decent cup of tea and you can't find PG tips (or don't want to spend a small fortune), **Tetley USA** products can sometimes be found in with the herbal teas. As with other less popular items, the trick is often to look at the very highest or the bottom shelves, so don't give up if it doesn't jump out at you from the first scan of the shelves! They do a **Tetley British Blend** (and a decaf version) that comes in a purple box. Personally, I don't find it as strong as I like (although, nowhere near as bad as Lipton), but it's a reasonable alternative.

Coffee

Conversely, if you are a coffee drinker you will be delighted with the quality and varieties of coffee available. Most American households have a coffee machine as standard, in the same way that we Brits own electric kettles (which are strangely absent in many homes in the US)! Therefore, the majority of coffee sold in the grocery stores is in the form of beans that you grind yourself or ground coffee. In some larger supermarkets you can even select your own beans and grind them in-store (the smell is delightful)! Popular brands include **Dunkin' Donuts**, **Green Mountain** & **Folgers**. Whilst you may be quite partial to a **Starbucks** Latte, their packaged ground coffee does not get great reviews.

Keurig brewing systems that use pre-filled pods to make individual coffees are extremely popular. Many people own these coffee machines or similar, and so there are a wide variety of pods available in stores.

Instant coffee is not very popular but you can buy some brands. Jars of instant coffee include **Nescafé** (sometimes called Nescafé Clasico and found in the Hispanic foods section although it is the same as the UK one) and **Folgers Classic Roast Instant Coffee**. However, instant coffee is more commonly available in individually packaged sachets or bags; **Starbucks VIA Ready Brew**, **Nescafe Tasters Choice Instant Coffee Sticks** and **Maxwell House Coffee Singles** are all popular brands.

Wot No Squash?!!!!

This is something that is totally lost in translation as you cross the Atlantic. Squash to an American is a pumpkin or marrow and you will get totally bemused looks if you try to explain the British definition of this word. You could try using the word cordial, or explaining that it is a juice concentrate that you dilute with water, but again, you are likely to draw blanks.

The closest thing available in the US market is powdered sachets of drinks mix… infamous **Kool-Aid** being the most popular brand. While Kool-Aid is well-known in popular culture as the drink used to mask the cyanide that killed nearly a 1000 cult members in the Jonestown Massacre of 1978 (hence the phrase "don't drink the Kool-Aid") it is still a very popular drink in the US. Individual sachets are mixed with water in a jug to create a fruit flavoured drink. Unfortunately, the mixes usually contain some worrisome artificial ingredients, particularly, artificial colours. Kool-Aid and other similar brands are well known for their tongue-staining ability! There are 'natural' alternatives made by brands such as **True Citrus**, who do lemon, orange, grapefruit and raspberry lemon flavoured mixes, all without artificial colours and preservatives.

Unfortunately, you may have kids like mine that simply prefer squash… proper British squash and nothing else.

In which case, never fear because you can buy **Robinson's squash** and **Ribena** in many supermarkets. Look in the international aisle and be prepared to pay 6 times more than you are used to in the UK! I justify it with the thought that I would spend much more on a bottle of wine for myself, so it only seems fair to indulge the children this way! Specialty and import supermarkets are often slightly cheaper and may do more varieties. Or you can sometimes get lucky and source it online (although shipping can often be costly because of the weight). As with the teabags, you can sometimes get it on subscription from Amazon, saving about 25% of the cost in stores.

Sodas
Instead of squash, many American families consume huge amounts of 'soda'… what we would call carbonated or 'fizzy' drinks. Fridge packs of soda cans are very popular and much cheaper than the UK.

Juice
Another popular soft drink in the US is juice. Apple juice is the drink of choice of most kids under the age of 10 compared to the UK where squash is *de rigueur*! Long-life juices made from concentrates are very common, but it is also possible to get fresh squeezed juices in the fridges. **Tropicana** is a popular brand.

Alcohol
In the UK, the full complement of alcoholic beverages can be purchased in supermarkets as long as you have ID to prove you are over 18 and you are buying within the licenced hours of sale. However, in the US there is still a slightly bizarre (post-prohibition?) attitude towards the purchase and consumption of booze and the regulations vary widely from state to state and even between counties and communities within states. Here in Houston, you can buy beer and wine in the supermarkets, but hard liquor (spirits as we Brits would say) must be purchased at a

Liquor Store. Elsewhere in Texas there are counties that are completely 'dry' and others are somewhat 'moist', only restricting the sale of beverages with more than 4% alcohol by volume. When you purchase alcohol in many parts of the US you will find that it is wrapped separately in a paper bag so that it is concealed from view, protecting the eyes of the innocent from corruption (and the illicit public drinker from the hand of the law thanks to the 4th amendment protecting them from being searched without a warrant)!

By contrast, in Louisiana you can buy booze 24 hours a day from supermarkets, pharmacies, convenience stores and petrol stations. You can also carry open containers of alcohol in public spaces (as long as the container isn't breakable) … they even have Drive-Thru Frozen Daiquiri Bars for goodness sake!

In all states, the minimum age of consumption & purchase of alcohol is 21 and the stores are very strict on their ID policy – my 60-something year old Mother-in-law even got asked to show her ID on one occasion, much to her delight! If you are under 30 you might as well get used to routinely carrying photo ID if you plan to buy alcohol at any time.

11 – SWEET TREATS AND SAVOURY SNACKS

Hersheys Schmershey… getting your mitts on *real* chocolate

Even most American's agree that European chocolate is far superior to its US counterpart. The very fact that we call it 'chocolate' rather than lumping it under the blandly generic term 'candy' as they do in America, speaks volumes! In fact, I'm totally bemused by the American love of **Hersheys** Candy as it is bitter and bizarre tasting in my opinion.

Thankfully, you can get hold of **Cadbury Dairy Milk** in the candy section of most supermarkets. In the US it is made by Hersheys but tastes waaaaaay better than Hersheys own brand bars. I'm sure that a direct comparison between UK Dairy Milk and US Dairy Milk chocolate would throw up some slight differences, but not enough to complain about in my opinion! It is sold in the large bar format, rather than in individual bars.

Other brands that sell good chocolate are **Lindt, Green & Blacks** and traditional American brand **Ghirardelli**. They have quality products that include some delicious dark chocolate, nut and filled varieties.

When it comes to individual chocolate bars there are some that will be instantly recognisable favourites from the UK. For example, **Snickers**, **Kit Kats**, **Rolos**, **Twix**, and **M&Ms** are all popular. There are also some other favourites that have very close equivalents:

- **Maltesers** – whilst the real things are occasionally available in the International section of the supermarket, a pretty decent alternative are called **Whoppers**.

- **Bounty** – the closest equivalent to this coconut chocolate favourite is known as **Mounds**.

- **Galaxy** – this popular chocolate is branded **Dove** in the US and has similar packaging as the UK.

- **Mars** – confusingly a **Milky Way** in the US (brown packaging instead of blue) is very similar to the UK favourite, Mars.

- **Milky Way** – to make things even more confusing, what we Brits know as a Milky Way is called a **3 Musketeers** (chocolate, because there are other flavours) bar.

This Christmas, I have been very excited to notice **Terry's Chocolate Oranges** in the mainstream supermarkets! As with the Cadbury's Chocolate available in the US, these are actually manufactured here in America by Hersheys. Thankfully, the difference in taste is subtle and barely noticeable!

Biscuits vs. Cookies

If you ask for biscuits in America what you will actually get is a flaky bread product very similar to an English scone. Rather than being made with butter like scones, they often use vegetable shortening or buttermilk and so are a little flakier and less sweet, but essentially the sort of thing you'd have served with clotted cream, jam and a pot of tea in Devon. In the US, particularly in the southern states, they are usually served with savoury dishes and gravy which sounded rather heathen to me until I tried it... it's delicious!

Biscuits to us Brits are what Americans refer to as either cookies or crackers (crackers are digestive-type biscuits and cookies are just about any other type). Oreos are the most popular type of multi-packed cookie and they do a number of varieties. **Oreo Chocolate Crème Cookies** are similar to a **bourbon biscuit** in as much as they are two chocolate biscuits sandwiched with chocolate goop in the middle! **Oreo Golden Cookies** are a reasonable substitute for **custard cream biscuits**. However, they do contain high fructose corn syrup for those who would wish to avoid it. **Newman's Own** produce an almost identical range of cookies using organic ingredients (you may need to look in the natural foods section of your supermarket to find these).

Pepperidge Farm produces a wide range of delicious biscuits and cookies. Their **Chessmen** biscuits are delicious **shortbread** style plain biscuits. They also produce the Australian favourite **Tim Tams**. For the uninitiated, these are very similar to the chocolate **Penguin** biscuits in the UK. Unfortunately, these have weirdly limited availability... you'll find them in Target (and sometimes Walmart) between the months of October and March only, so stock up while you can!

Animal crackers are a very popular type of biscuit, especially for children who love the animal shapes of these cookies. They are similar to **digestive** biscuits. **Barnum's** is the original brand but many other varieties are available, some even in a chocolate variety.

For those of you with a particular fondness for British biscuits, you can buy some of the more popular varieties in the International aisle of the supermarket. **McVities Digestives** and **Hob Nobs**, **Jammie Dodgers** and **custard creams** are frequently seen. They are expensive and unless they are obviously imported British brands (like McVities) I've found that they are usually cheap-tasting and inferior US imitations.

Although not technically biscuits, granola type bars are very popular in the US and make great lunchbox fillers. **Cascadian Farm Organic Chewy Granola Bars** and **Clif Kid Z-bars** are both excellent.

Crisps vs. Chips

In the US, what we call **crisps** are known as **potato chips** and what we call chips are known as **French fries**! It can cause some confusion, so be prepared!

Potato chips are very popular, but are usually only sold in large bags. Multi-packs of individually bagged packets of crisps are not as common as they are in the UK. If you walk down the crisps aisle of the supermarket, the majority are huge family-sized bags. You can find small lunch-box sized bags in multi-packs and these are commonly available from the brand **Lay's**. This is the American name for **Walker's**. The flavours available are also somewhat limited with salted, cheese and (occasionally) salt & vinegar being the usual selection. Sadly, you won't find British favourite flavours such as cheese & onion, pickled onion, bacon, steak etc...

Kettle chips & tortilla crisps are very popular and often dominate the snack section of the supermarket. **Cape Cod** Kettle chips are a popular brand.

UK favourites such as **Wotsits** aren't available, but a similar puffed corn cheese snack product is made by **Pirate's Booty**.

Unfortunately, for products like **Monster Munch** and **Prawn Cocktail Skips** you will have to go to a British import store (online is often the only place to get them).

Fruit snacks

Fruit based snacks are popular with children and they have the popular **Betty Crocker Fruit Roll-Ups** (with questionable amounts of fruit!) which are virtually identical to **Kellogg's Fruit Winders** in the UK. Another popular brand of fruit snacks is **Welch's**. For a more natural alternative without artificial colours or flavours, try **Annie's Homegrown Organic Bunny Fruit Snacks**. Made from organic fruit purées, **Clif Kid Fruit Ropes** are tasty and popular too.

Pretzels & other savoury snacks

Pretzels (the hard, crispy ones rather than the larger doughy ones) are very popular in the US and are a common snack for adults and children alike. **Snyder's of Hanover** is the leading pretzel company in the United States (one of the leading snack companies all round in fact). They do a variety of pretzels in different shapes and bag sizes, from jumbo family-sized to small lunchbox sized mini bags!

Another hugely popular snack in the US is **popcorn** and not just as a treat at the cinema. **Orville Redenbacher's Naturals** range of microwave bags is good, free from artificial ingredients and also does a low salt version. However, do yourself a favour and pop your own corn in a paper lunch bag in the microwave rather than spend a fortune on pre-packaged microwave popcorn!

Pepperidge Farm Goldfish, one of the most popular snacks for children in the US, is a huge favourite with many families. On the plus side, they are deliciously cheesy and contain no artificial colourings, flavourings or preservatives and there is also a wholegrain variety.

However, as with many savoury processed snacks they are very salty… at 250mg per serving they contain 25% of the daily recommended amount of sodium for toddlers, 20% for school age children and 10% for adults!

As a US brand that many Brits will be familiar with **Ritz crackers** (and the Ritz Cheese sandwich biscuits) are popular, however, as with many processed foods in the States the recipe is slightly different to the UK containing High Fructose Corn Syrup (HFCS) in place of sugar. A brand that produces similar crackers with organic ingredients is **Late July** and their Classic Rich crackers are almost identical to Ritz (the **Late July Mini Cheddar Cheese Bite Size Sandwich Crackers** are good too). As with the Goldfish crackers, these snacks are quite high in sodium.

Water biscuits for cheese are available but are known as **Table Water Crackers**. **Carr's** is a popular brand. **Jacob's cream crackers** are unfortunately only available in the international section of the supermarket or in specialty import supermarkets. However, Jewish **matzo** is similar (but a larger version) and is usually available in the International foods section with the other kosher food items.

Ryvita Crispbread is readily available but their lighter, wheat **Crackerbread** is only available in the UK. A very similar alternative is made by **Wasa** and called **Crisp 'n' Light 7 Grain Crispbread**.

Ice cream
You will be delighted to know that both **Ben & Jerry's** and **Häagen-Dazs** are available and very popular ice creams. **Breyers Ice cream** has been a popular brand for over 100 years and has always prided itself on using natural ingredients. In recent years, some of their newer lines have started to include some artificial ingredients, but their original ice cream range has a delicious **Natural Vanilla**

ice cream containing reassuringly familiar ingredients like milk, cream, sugar and vanilla! Here in Texas, and other southern states, **Blue Bell Creameries** ice cream is also hugely popular (interestingly, even though it's only sold in 20 states, it's America's 3rd bestselling ice cream which says a lot about Texans' love of ice cream). Their range does include natural & artificial flavourings, and high fructose corn syrup. However, if you are concerned about things like that bear in mind that they carry 3 different flavours of vanilla… and their **Natural Vanilla Bean** flavour (the one with the brown rim on the lid) uses only natural flavours and no HFCS!

Something significant to note is that what we call a **sorbet** (fruit-based ice dessert) is often called a **sherbet** in the US. This isn't actually factually correct as for a manufacturer to label a food 'sherbet' in the US it must contain a small amount of dairy ingredients (between 1 and 2%). Any more than 2% dairy and it will be called a frozen dairy dessert. Sorbets with fruit only are sometimes called **Italian ices**.

Other popular US frozen desserts include the square **Klondike Bar** with its silver paper wrapper and polar bear logo. It is quite similar to a choc ice bar. **Nestlé Dibs** are also popular with kids (and adults). These are small, bite-sized chunks of ice cream dipped in chocolate and sometimes nuts.

12 – BABIES & KIDS

When we moved to the US in 2010, one of the biggest sources of anxiety for me was making sure that the transition was as easy as possible for our children. Finding a school, playgroup, friends and activities was just the tip of the iceberg. Our kids are quite fussy eaters and with the overseas move looming I had also allowed our 17 month old twins to continue using their bottles for their bedtime milk… I figured that any additional form of familiar comfort would be a benefit. Consequently, I was keen to find familiar foods and snacks to keep my jetlagged and unsettled brood happy. It was not as easy you'd imagine.

Formula, bottles & teats
I have had to rely on my trusted expat playgroup friends for the advice in this section. My own children were thankfully drinking cow's milk by the time we moved to the States so finding formula was never one of my concerns.

Formula milk manufactured in the US is stringently controlled by the US FDA (Food & Drug Administration), and as such can be relied on to be of a good quality. As in the UK there are varying types of formula available: powdered, ready to drink, liquid concentrate etc… There are also a wide number of brands to choose from but only a few that are consistently recommended. I have listed them in terms of popularity:

- **Enfamil (Mead Johnson)** – This brand is considered the closest to the UK favourite **Aptamil**. It is a popular brand and is frequently recommended by paediatricians and health officials. I used an anti-regurgitation formula produced by Enfamil when we lived in the UK (imported and on prescription) as my twins had severe reflux and we found it brilliant. Expat friends of ours have used both Aptamil in the UK and Enfamil here in the US and have found the transition easy. In addition to their normal infant & toddler formulas Enfamil has a range of milks for specific requirements such as prematurity, colic, lactose-intolerance, reflux, multiple allergies, older baby and more. One expat mum I spoke to raved about their pre-measured 4oz packets for convenience when out-and-about! Their website www.enfamil.com provides more details.
- **Similac (Abbot)** – Another popular brand and one also frequently recommended by paediatricians. The difference between Enfamil and Similac is minimal and it is really down to a case of personal preference, as with Coke or Pepsi! In fact, some parents I spoke to switched happily between the two depending on what was on offer! Similac offer a full range of products for different needs just as Enfamil. However, Similac also produces a USDA Organic formula that is therefore produced without the rBST growth hormones discussed in chapter 3. See their website for more information

https://similac.com/baby-formula.

- **Gerber Good Start (Nestlé)** – Gerber is a popular brand of baby food/formula, with a variety of types available. More information on their products can be found on their website www.gerber.com/birth/products/formula.aspx.

Regardless of the brand you choose, do read the instructions carefully as some brands have different preparation methods than in the UK, for example, one scoop of formula to 2 fl oz of water (rather than the 1:1 ratio usual in the UK).

It is possible to buy imported UK brands but you will find that they are expensive (see chapter 16 for more information on sources). Saying that, one of the things mentioned to me by several of the expats I spoke to was the high price of all infant formulas here in the US compared to the UK, with a tub of normal formula powder costing around $25 on average. Many of the grocery stores do offers so it is worth looking for these, and coupons are available from most of the manufacturer's websites too! One expat mum explained that she had barely had to buy any formula, as she had been given several full-sized cartons as samples by her baby's paediatrician… so it's worth asking!

With regard to bottles & teats, there are a number of brands available that are also popular in the UK including **Phillips Avent**, **Dr Brown**, **MAM** and **NUK**. However, if your child is stuck on a particular UK type of bottle it may be worth investigating availability and stocking up on replacement teats prior to your move. Our twins were used to the **Tommee Tippee Closer to Nature** bottles and the replacement teats were difficult to find in the grocery stores and I had to source them online.

Baby food & snacks
As with the baby formula, the recommendations in this

section come from my playgroup friends! The following brands (some familiar from the UK) are popular:

- **Ella's kitchen** – this brand will be familiar to many Brits. Their squeezable pouches of 100% organic purees and smoothies have become an instant success since being introduced to the US market in August 2011. Many supermarkets now carry this brand including Kroger and Target, but you can also buy online from places such as Amazon and Diapers.com or direct from the Ella's Kitchen website. www.ellaskitchen.com

- **Happy Babies (and Happy Tot for older babies)** – this brand also produces squeezable pouches of purees suitable for weaning babies, however, the brand was commonly recommended for its popular baby friendly snacks. Many Brit expat mums I spoke to bemoan the fact that the **Organix** brand of baby food isn't sold in stores here in the US, especially for their great baby snacks. The Happy Baby brand was mentioned by several mums as being a good alternative; their Rice cakes and Happy Puffs were particularly popular (and are both sweetened with apple juice rather than cane sugar). www.happybabyfood.com/

- **Plum Organic** – This is not the same as the Plum Baby range in the UK, despite the same name (and even fairly similar branding); however, the companies do have a similar ethos and range of products. www.plumorganics.com/

- **Sprout** – Another brand recommended for its organic range of pouches of baby purees and cereals. http://www.sproutbabyfood.com/

- **Beech Nut** – a long-established and trusted brand of baby foods. www.beechnut.com/index.asp

- **Gerber** – this is the leading brand of baby and

toddler food products in the US. In addition to their standard products, they have introduced an organic range. www.gerber.com

- **Baby Mum Mums** – a popular alternative to rusks, these rice cake teething biscuits and snacks are well recommended, in particular the banana flavour ones as they have less than 1g of sugar per biscuit. www.mummums.com

For those parents who have babies particularly attached to UK brands of baby food (the **Organix** range of **Goodies snacks** was frequently mentioned) you can obtain them on the internet although shipping costs are often high. Try http://www.britishcornershop.co.uk/ and Amazon.

Other kids' items

I know toothpaste is not a food, but I felt it was definitely worth mentioning as it has been a difficult issue for us here in the States. Most children's toothpastes in the US are fruit or bubble gum flavoured and my boys had grown accustomed to the **Aquafresh Milk Teeth** mild mint-flavoured type in the UK. Cue tantrums every tooth-brushing when we first moved here! Admittedly, the idea of brushing my teeth with pink & sparkly bubble gum toothpaste isn't very appealing either! There are a couple of brands that do mint flavoured toothpastes for older kids such as **Sensodyne Pronamel in Gentle Mint** (suitable for children aged 2 years and up), **Aquafresh Kids Fluoride Toothpaste in Bubble Mint** (again, suitable for 2 years+) and **Colgate Fresh 'n' Protect** (it is marketed for ages 8+, although on the back it says suitable for age 2+ if a pea-sized amount is used with adult supervision). For toddlers under the age of 2, the only brand of mint flavoured toothpaste I have found is a natural tooth gel produced by **Weleda** and available online or in 'natural' or 'whole' food stores. Personally, we found it easiest to stock up on our favourite Milk Teeth Toothpaste when we had visitors from the UK!

Also, **paracetamol** is not available in the US, but there is a very similar drug called **acetaminophen**. For infant suspensions, the most common and popular brand is **Tylenol** (to the point where the generic name for the drug is often not used). Unfortunately, in recent years the Tylenol brand (manufactured by Johnson & Johnson's) has been recalled several times from stores over various concerns from unexpected metal shavings, odd odours, contamination of the manufacturing plant with bacteria and problems with their dosing method. Subsequently, there is not a huge amount of confidence in this brand at the moment and many expat families choose to stock up on trusty **Calpol** from back in the UK. Infant **ibuprofen** is available under the brand names **Advil** or **Motrin** and is a handy alternative for pain and fever relief.

13 – SHOPPING FOR RESTRICTED DIETS

I am very grateful to have a family that (fussiness aside) can eat most things I put in front of them. We have no known food allergies or intolerances and so this has thankfully never been an issue for us in doing our grocery shopping. For those with specific or restricted dietary needs, moving to a new country and away from the familiar must be an especially daunting time. I therefore felt it was important to include a section on this in the book and was able to call on some of my friends and contacts here in Houston to supply me with the information necessary!

A lot of mainstream supermarkets have 'Free From' sections catering to a range of dietary restrictions. Gluten free is particularly 'popular' in part because of the perceived weight loss benefit of adopting this type of diet … and American's seem to love their 'diet' programmes! Dairy-free, and sugar-free products are also well catered for. Many of the more 'natural' and 'whole-food' oriented stores seem to stock a wider range of these types of products so they're worth perusing first. One English lady

I spoke to said that the range of 'free from' products available in mainstream stores here in Texas had surprised her and there was a much wider selection available than in the UK. Not really knowing much about this subject myself, I have simply provided a list of brands and products recommended to me.

Dairy free brands

There are a wide variety of non-dairy milks, yoghurts, cheeses, spreads and other products. Popular brands include:

- **Taste the Dream** – this company started out with its popular range Rice Dream back in the 1970s. They do ranges of rice, soy, almond and coconut milk products including long-life and refrigerated milk and ice cream. www.tastethedream.com
- **Whole Soy & Co** – a range of tasty soy yoghurts, including plain and fruit flavours. www.wholesoyco.com
- **Stonyfield** – this popular brand of dairy products carries a line of soy yoghurts called O'Soy www.stonyfield.com/products/stonyfield/soy-yogurt
- **Silk** – the most common brand of soy milk available. http://silksoymilk.com
- **Westsoy** – Another brand of soy milk. www.westsoymilk.com
- **Tofutti** – this brand produces a range of dairy/lactose free cream cheeses, sour cream, and frozen desserts. www.tofutti.com
- **So Delicious** – most popular for their coconut and almond milk ice cream varieties, this brand also produces dairy free milk, coffee creamers,

yoghurts and frozen ice lollies.
http://sodeliciousdairyfree.com

- **Earth Balance** – this brand is most well known for their vegan soy-based 'butter' spread. However, they also do a lactose and egg free mayonnaise dressing.
  www.earthbalancenatural.com
- **Veggie** – this brand is well known for its vegan cheeses, including cheddar, mozzarella and parmesan equivalents.
  www.goveggiefoods.com
- **Road's End Organics** – this brand started out with its popular dairy/lactose-free Mac 'n' Cheese.
  www.edwardandsons.com/reo_info.itml
- **Amy's** – this brand can frequently be found in the freezer section of the 'whole' or 'natural' foods section of your mainstream supermarket. They do dairy/lactose/gluten free ready meals like Mac 'n' Cheese, lasagne, burritos and pizzas.
  http://www.amys.com

I was also given another piece of advice to pass on for parents of young children with dairy allergies, particularly those with low weight. In the UK, some children have non-dairy milk formulas prescribed by their doctors to ensure they are getting sufficient nutrition; a common brand is **Neocate**. This is available in the US without prescription, but is very expensive ($40+ per can). It could be that your medical insurer will help towards costs, but not guaranteed, and this varies from state to state. The Neocate website provides more details on how to apply for reimbursement (www.neocate.com/reimbursement). You may also want to consider stocking up in the UK prior to your move here.

Gluten free brands
Again, there is usually a section of the supermarket

dedicated to Gluten free products, but some brands can be found in the regular aisles. It is also worth investigating local bakeries as you may find one that specialises in Gluten Free products, for example, here in Texas we have Gluten Free Houston (http://glutenfreehouston.com/)... Definitely worth the effort of locating for a special occasion cake! The following Gluten Free brands are recommended:

- **The Pure Pantry** – this brand makes an All-Purpose Baking Mix that can be used in place of flour in most recipes and it comes very well recommended. Their baking mixes for cakes, cookies and pancakes are also popular.
  http://thepurepantry.com/
- **King Arthur Flour** – this popular mainstream brand of flour and bread products also produces a range of gluten free flours and baking mixes.
  http://www.kingarthurflour.com/glutenfree/
- **Cherrybrook Kitchen** – a brand of cake and cookie mixes.
  www.cherrybrookkitchen.com
- **De Boles** – a gluten free pasta range.
  www.deboles.com/products/gluten-free-products.php
- **Tinkyada** – a rice-based pasta range.
  www.tinkyada.com
- **Ancient Harvest** – a quinoa-based range of pastas and polenta.
  www.quinoa.net
- **Hodgson Mill** – this brand has a range of GF flours, bread, cake and pancake mixes (including pizza dough) and a range of rice-based pasta.
  www.hodgsonmillstore.com/en/Gluten-Free/Gluten-Free.aspx
- **Edward & Sons** – the same company that sells dairy-free Mac 'n' Cheese also does a number of

GF products including rice snacks, condiments (teriyaki and Worcestershire sauces) and even GF ice cream cones!
www.edwardandsons.com/specialdiets_celiac.itml

- **Ener-G** – a brand of GF bread familiar to those from the UK.
www.ener-g.com

- **Food for life** – this brand produces a wide selection of GF bread products including tortillas and English Muffins.
www.foodforlife.com

- **Glutino** – this brand specialises only in Gluten Free products and has ranges of breads, snacks, frozen meals, cereals and baking mixes.
www.glutino.com/our-products

- **Lundberg** – another brand of GF pasta and snacks.
www.lundberg.com/Products/Special_diets/Glutenfree.aspx

- **Nature's Path EnviroKidz** – have a range of GF cereals and snacks.
http://us.naturespath.com/our-products

- **Udi's** – a well recommended brand of GF bread products that includes bagels, ready-made pizza crusts, burger & hotdog buns.
http://udisglutenfree.com/product-catalog/

- **Schär** – another brand specialising in GF products such as pastas, breads, mixes and more.
www.schar.com/us/gluten-free-products

Vegetarian/Vegan
Many of the dairy free products listed above are suitable for vegans. The following brands of meat substitute products are commonly available:

- **Quorn** – a very popular brand, familiar from the UK. Found in the freezer section. - www.quorn.us

- **Lightlife Smart** – a common brand often seen in the fridges next to the produce section (with the tofu). They have a range of hotdogs, burgers, chicken, minced meat and deli meat substitutes, plus ready meals.
  www.lightlife.com/Vegan-Food-Vegetarian-Diet
- **Morningstar Farms** – their veggie burgers come well recommended!
  www.morningstarfarms.com
- **Nasoya** – a popular brand of Tofu. Usually found next to the salad fridge in the produce section or with the 'organic' and 'natural' dairy foods.
  www.nasoya.com/index.html

14 – HOUSEHOLD & CLEANING ITEMS

I didn't set out to include non-food items in this book, but as I've been writing it I realised that most people buy their cleaning and household products in the supermarket while grocery shopping and that there are a few differences that it's worth knowing about.

Laundry detergents

One thing many Brits bemoan is the poor quality of the appliances in the US. Getting used to the huge capacity top loading machines is yet another thing acclimatise to and I have to say that I have found them nowhere near as efficient as my old Hotpoint front-loading washer in the UK. It also took me a while to find a replacement laundry detergent as I have sensitive, hives-prone skin which is often irritated by harsh cleaning products. On my first supermarket trip here in the US, I spent an agonising 15 minutes scanning all the laundry detergents in the store looking for any brand that said non-biological, only to be disappointed as this is not a term used in America. In fact, you will find that you have to read the labels to check whether any enzymes have been added to the formula. Ones that definitely <u>do</u> have enzymes added include **Arm**

& Hammer Essentials, **Ultra Plus**, **Tide Original**, **Tide Pure Essentials** and **Tide Stain Release** (powder, not liquid). Do check carefully if you are sensitive to these ingredients as the formulas do change.

Thankfully, many brands (including the ones above) also have a product line labelled Free & Clear. These are hypoallergenic versions free from colours, fragrances and additives known to irritate sensitive skins. The most popular brand of hypoallergenic laundry products, and one recommended by dermatologists, is **All Free & Clear**.

Eco-friendly brands of cleaning supplies

For the purpose of this book, I am focusing on eco-friendly and natural cleaning products lines. Again, it is folks like me with sensitive skin that will have specific needs in mind when selecting cleaning products so I thought I would just cover these. **Seventh Generation** and **Method** are the two most commonly found 'natural' ranges of cleaning products, and these are easily found in most supermarkets. The very popular brand **Clorox** that produces standard bleach and disinfectant products (and are as popular in the US as brands like **Dettol** and **Domestos** in the UK), also has a range of 'natural' cleaning products called **Green Works**. Their multi-surface spray is popular and readily available. Another brand, **Mrs Meyer's Clean Day** has a great selection of cleaning and hygiene products that are made from essential oils and have very distinctive traditional packaging.

15 – CHRISTMAS & OTHER HOLIDAYS

It is often at seasonal holidays that we expats struggle the most being away from 'home'. Aside from missing family & friends, there is something about the familiar foods and traditions that are comforting. Christmas just wouldn't be Christmas without a mince pie and the naff jokes and hats out of a cracker! The difficulty is that the American traditions for Christmas (and other holidays) are different to our own. For example, in most American households they do not serve turkey or goose for Christmas dinner, having only just surfaced from their Turkey-induced comas from Thanksgiving a month before. Traditionally, families eat ham or roast beef, or another family favourite. They also (sadly) do not have the mince pies and mulled wine tradition; rather, the somewhat unappetisingly named eggnog is the traditional drink served with nibbles.

However, do not despair as it is possible to rustle up your seasonal favourites if you look hard and plan ahead!

Christmas

One handy hint I will pass on is to buy your Turkey for Christmas in the week after Thanksgiving and freeze it for Christmas! You will save a fortune as there is frequently an excess of this poultry in stores following Thanksgiving and the fresh ones go on sale! Another tip is to try the American tradition of brining your Turkey prior to cooking... delicious! For detailed instructions on this technique search online for Alton Brown's recipe and look up his "Good Eats" show on You Tube for step-by-step, idiot-proof brining. He's quite annoying to watch, but the brine really does make all the difference. One uniquely American method of cooking turkey is probably best avoided for novices and that is deep frying the bird whole... apparently this method is responsible for $15 million worth of insurance claims in the US every year!

One of my husband's favourite accompaniments to Christmas dinner has got to be **Pigs in Blankets**. In Britain, these are made from chipolata sausages, wrapped in streaky bacon. In the US however, this term is used to describe hot dogs wrapped in ready-made biscuit (the American scone type) dough. Not the same, at all! In fact, **chipolata sausages** in the US are rarely seen outside specialist butchers, so it's quite a challenge all round! However, I have substituted the readily available **pork breakfast links** (see the section on sausages in chapter 6) for chipolatas in this recipe and it has worked out deliciously! You can even make cocktail sized versions by gently twisting the breakfast links in the middle a few times and then cutting with scissors.

The rest of the main meal is relatively straight forward to source. **Brussels sprouts** are common in the supermarkets, but you may struggle to obtain **parsnips**. See my earlier sections in chapter 9 on roast dinner accompaniments and stocks/gravies for more information on things like gravy, stuffing, cranberry and bread sauce.

For traditional festive baking you may struggle to get some of the ingredients. One of the most difficult things to find is decent **mincemeat**. I was delighted in my first year living in Texas to discover large jars of **Robertson's**

Classic Mincemeat in my local grocery store. However, when it was opened and tasted I was severely disappointed. Despite being made in the UK it is actually a version manufactured for the US market and distributed by GFI of Westport, CT. It is much sweeter than the UK version, containing corn syrup, and has a much wetter, sloppier consistency. It's also lighter brown in colour. It really is not *that* unpleasant but is significantly different to what us Brits are used to and does not compare well. Other US brands such as **Crosse & Blackwell** & **Borden's None Such** are even worse and should probably be avoided.

Thankfully, it is possible to obtain imported UK versions of mincemeat (prepared for the UK market). Look online as places like Amazon and some of the British food suppliers will have them available, but be prepared to spend more than you would in the UK. A list of online suppliers is in chapter 16.

You can also make your own mincemeat (which I recommend anyway, as it's very easy and delicious). Try Delia Smith's classic recipe, available online. However, this in itself poses some problems as the ingredients you need for homemade mincemeat, and other festive baked goods such as Christmas cake and pudding, can be difficult to source and expensive too:

- **Stem ginger** is a tricky one to find. I was offered crystallised ginger in the baking aisle, pickled sushi ginger in the Asian section and ginger marmalade by a very helpful shop assistant in my local store, none of which were what I was after. You can buy stem ginger, but you will need to ask for ginger in syrup. An American brand is **Roland**. I found some in a specialty import food store in Houston called Phoenicia. It's worth trying specialist delis and ethnic supermarkets for unusual ingredients. Alternatively, look online.

- **Candied peel** is another difficult one. During the Holiday season in the US, the supermarkets fill up with seasonal baking supplies including **candied fruit** for use in baking. Personally, I would avoid these neon multi-coloured monstrosities at all costs. It is not the same as candied peel and contains all sorts of additives and artificial colours. It is essentially like gummy fruit sweets and bears no resemblance to real fruit. Try whole foods markets and specialty stores/delis and you can find candied peel. Candied peel is sometimes called **glacé peel**. You can of course make your own and it's quite straightforward. There are lots of recipes available online.

- **Glacé cherries**, usually called **candied cherries** in the US, are easier to find. However, as in the UK, the ones you buy in the main supermarkets are often full of lots of artificial colours and additives. Look for naturally coloured alternatives at whole foods grocery stores.

- **Currants** and **sultanas** are not very common in the general supermarkets, with **raisins** and **dried cranberries** dominating the shelves. In fact, it's because the term 'raisin' is used to describe the dried fruit of nearly all grape varieties, whereas we Brits differentiate between the varieties; sultanas coming from white sultana grapes, and currants from the small black Corinth variety. You may find currants labelled somewhat confusingly as **Black Currant Raisins** (not to be confused with dried blackcurrants), **Zante Currants** or **Corinthian Raisins**. Sultanas are sometimes labelled as golden raisins.

- The closest thing to **Marzipan** available in the mainstream supermarkets in the US is called **almond paste** and the difference in taste and appearance is minimal. It has a slightly coarser texture and contains whole egg rather than just the whites like marzipan. You can find marzipan in more specialty stores and ethnic supermarkets, but unless you are a connoisseur the difference doesn't warrant the effort.

- Suet and mixed spice are discussed in greater detail in the store cupboard basics chapter.

Whilst not a food item, no Christmas dinner table is complete without the crackers. And I don't mean the edible ones! These aren't part of the American tradition and will need explaining to many Americans! However, even just in the last few years I have seen them more frequently available. If you are struggling to get hold of them in your grocery store, look in craft stores like **Michaels** or in home décor stores such as **Pier One** instead.

Easter

Easter is a big deal in America and the tradition of the Easter Bunny is right up there with good ol' Santa. In fact, Easter egg hunts are so very popular that you commonly see sets of plastic eggs ready to fill with small candies just for this purpose. Another popular treat is a marshmallow chick made by **Peeps**. This is in contrast to the UK where a child may get one large chocolate egg filled with some sweets. As with Halloween, much of the bulk candy available for Easter is pretty cheap and nasty, but you can buy some familiar items such as the iconic **Lindt chocolate bunny** and **Cadbury's mini eggs**.

Unfortunately, many of the culinary associations that we Brits have with Easter are not shared on this other side of the Atlantic. **Lamb** is a rarely seen meat in the mainstream supermarkets and isn't eaten traditionally on Easter Sunday as it is in the UK (read more in chapter 6). **Simnel cake** is also not an American tradition at Easter. As at Christmas, finding **marzipan** for the apostles can be tricky, but look for **almond paste** in the baking section. And most sadly of all, **Hot Cross Buns** are also not enjoyed by American's at Easter (they don't know what they're missing)! Making them yourself is the best hope you can have of enjoying this treat, so look up Nigella Lawson's great recipe!

Whilst occurring a whole 40 days prior to Easter, I ought to mention **Shrove Tuesday** also has very different traditions in the US where it associated with **Mardi Gras** (literally translated as 'Fat Tuesday') carnivals rather than **pancakes**! Don't forget that American pancakes are different to the thin crepes we Brits mean. A pancake in the US is more like a drop scone, so that is worth considering if you are using an American recipe or pancake mix.

16 – BRITISH STUFF YOU JUST CAN'T DO WITHOUT - AND WAYS TO GET IT

I feel that I have adapted well to the food available here in the US and adjusted my culinary repertoire accordingly, but sometimes there really isn't any substitute for one of your British favourites unavailable in the US mainstream. In these circumstances, it can be a bit frustrating, especially if you have a favourite recipe that just isn't the same without xyz ingredient! There are ways to get the majority of items you need.

Bringing food from the UK

Getting through US immigration can be a long and quite intimidating process as it is, but the matter is complicated when considering bringing some of your British favourite foods with you in your luggage. It is widely believed that you cannot bring food products into the US from abroad and so many people either don't bother trying or risk incurring the wrath of immigration control (plus a $10,000 fine) by sneaking in food illicitly. However, it is not strictly true. According to the US Customs and Border Protection Agency (US CBP):

> *"You may be able to bring in food such as fruits, meats or other agricultural products depending on the region or country from which you are traveling. Restrictions are placed on these products to protect community health, preserve the environment and prevent the introduction of devastating diseases to domestic plants and animals".*

The important thing to remember is that **failure to declare food products can result in up to $10,000 in fines and penalties.** The US CBP website help section lists items that are generally admissible:

- https://help.cbp.gov/app/answers/detail/a_id/82/search/1

In summary, most foods that are manufactured in the UK, unopened and labelled in English are admissible, including condiments, sauces, fish, fruit preserves, teabags, baked goods (such as cookies/cakes), cheese, candy & chocolate, dried fruits, canned goods, infant formula, dried herbs and spices, and flour.

The biggest exception to this rule is anything containing meat, poultry and eggs. Unfortunately, that includes meat gravy powders, dried soup mixes and stock cubes. Also, there are restrictions on things like fruits and vegetables, cottage cheese, goats milk and goats milk products, rice, certain varieties of loose tea leaves (such as citrus), dried spices containing seeds and/or citrus leaves. Check in advance to make sure that the items you are bringing in are admissible, or they will be confiscated.

The important thing to bear in mind is that you **MUST** declare the items you are bringing in. When you go through immigration, the customs official will go through your declaration. If you have indicated that you are bringing food in, you will be asked to list the items. Once you have collected your baggage, your bags will be scanned (and maybe inspected) to make sure that the items you have listed are evident. It can add a bit of time to your transit through the airport, but better that than incurring the wrath of the US CBP!

The International Aisle in your supermarket

Mentioned a gazillion times already in this book, the international aisle of your supermarket will become a vital source of some British favourites you simply can't do without. As in UK supermarkets, one section is usually dedicated to foods from around the world, and often split into regions. In the UK you will usually see Indian, Mexican, and Asian foods grouped together. In the US, there are often British, Asian, Hispanic, Indian, Caribbean, and Kosher foods down the international aisle. One thing to bear in mind is that as imports, many of these foods are very expensive.

International, import and specialty grocery stores

Another source of British favourites I have mentioned liberally throughout this book is the international or specialty supermarket. The easiest way to find one in your area is to do a Google search for 'International supermarket in …' or 'Specialty supermarket in…'. Doing this search for Houston where I live throws up a list of some great places including:

- Phoenicia Speciality Foods
  www.phoeniciafoods.com
- Fiesta Mart
  www.fiestamart.com
- Leibman's
  www.leibmans.com
- Trader Joe's
  www.traderjoes.com

British Stores – chintz & teapots anyone?
Here in Houston is a shop called the British Isles Store.
On my first visit, I was quite surprised to consider that the
things most associated with us Brits are so clichéd! Wall-
to-wall teapots, Denby, tartan, doilies and Cath Kidston-
esque chintz! Once the initial surprise had passed, I then
proceeded to spend a delightful hour browsing through
their well-stocked food section. As with all imports, be
prepared to pay A LOT! Sometimes, these things are just
worth it! It is especially nice for the occasional treat like a
Cadbury's Caramel Easter Egg or some proper sausages!

Online
These days the internet has made it much easier to track
down British food favourites from the comfort of your
own home! Again, the cost (plus the shipping costs) can
be high, but in other cases you can actually save money.

For example, you can set up regular deliveries of grocery
items through the **Amazon.com Subscribe & Save
scheme** and save 15% straight away. This is great for
popular items such as Heinz Baked Beans and PG Tips tea
bags. You simply stipulate how many you want and how
often, and a regular order is sent to you.

There are many online shops specialising in British Food
stuffs. It's worth looking around at prices and seeing if
there are special offers:

- www.britishfood.com
- www.britishdelights.com
- www.britishcornershop.co.uk
- www.britishaisles.com
- www.britishfoodshop.com
- www.britishfooddepot.com

See the section on bacon in chapter 6 for online sources of
British meat products.

17 – SURVIVING YOUR FIRST FEW DAYS

The first few hours in a new country are understandably stressful and for those travelling with a family it can be particularly unsettling. We arrived in the US late afternoon on Easter Sunday and if it weren't for the fact that my Uncle was living in Houston and could drive me around to find the one supermarket open on this holiday, we would have had some pretty grumpy toddlers who didn't have some milk for their jet-lagged (very) early morning start! Many expats get assigned to temporary corporate lets, furnished self-catering apartments reserved by companies to use for temporary stays. In the month or so that it takes to find somewhere to live and have your container of furniture arrive from home, it is certainly a preferable option to staying in a hotel. However, the first jet-lagged few days can be hard, especially without supplies. The aim of this list is to get you enough things to tide you over for a few days until you get your bearings. It is designed with families in mind, but I figured that most expats *sans enfant* would not be worried about this sort of thing and would happily eat out for a few days.

For a more convenient printout version of this list, complete with photos of the items for easy identification, go to:

- http://www.mamawithideas.com/p/british-expats-guide-to-grocery.html.

The English translation is in *italics* where appropriate (just as a reminder when you are no doubt jet-lagged and/or haven't read the whole book yet). Recommended brands/items are in **bold**. Items marked with an * are pretty good alternatives to some of the items in the International section if not available.

Produce Section
- Fruit/s of choice
- Bag of carrots/other fresh vegetables
- English seedless cucumber
- Potatoes, russet
- Onions
- Pint of tomatoes, baby plum (*cherry tomatoes*)
- Bag of washed salad

Artisan Bread/Bakery Section
- "Homestyle" white bread
  or, Whole wheat sliced bread
  (ask for slicing if necessary)

Artisan Cheese section
- Sharp cheddar (mature) - **Cabot**

Butcher/Meat section
- Pack of pork breakfast links (*small chipolata-style sausages*) – **Jimmy Dean Original Links**
- Chicken tenderloins (*breasts*)
- Ground beef (*minced beef*)

Deli fridge section
- Pack of sandwich ham – **Hormel Natural Choice Cooked Deli Ham**

Alcohol section
- Beer – **Shiner** is a good Texas beer!
- Wine
- Champagne to celebrate your arrival!

Beverages section
- Apple juice – **Mott's for Tots**
- Instant coffee – **Nescafé Clasico**
  or, Ground coffee for machine (don't forget the filters) – **Dunkin' Donut Original**
- Teabags* – **Tetley British Blend**

Snacks section
- Cookies (*biscuits*) - **Pepperidge Farm Chessmen** are like plain shortbread
- Potato chips (*crisps*) – **Lay's Classic Potato Chips 6-count Singles**
- Cheese-y crackers - **Pepperidge Farm Goldfish**

Cans, Bottles & Jars section
- Canned tomatoes, diced
- Canned corn
- Canned tuna – **Starkist Solid White Albacore in Water**
- Marinara pasta sauce – **Prego**
- Tomato ketchup – **Heinz Simply Ketchup**

Pasta & Rice section
- Pasta
- Rice

International section
- Squash – **Robinson's** or **Ribena**
- Tea bags – **PG Tips**
- Baked beans – **Heinz**
- Cereal – **Weetabix** (sometimes available in normal cereal section)

Dairy fridge section (there may be a separate 'Organic' dairy fridge)
- Brown cage-free eggs (*free range*)
- Organic 2% Milk (*semi-skimmed*) – **Horizon**
- Whipped butter (*spreadable butter*) – **Land O Lakes**
- Kids' yogurts – **Stoneyfield YoKids** or **YoBaby**
- Fresh orange juice – **Simply Orange**

Cereal section
- Cheerios - **Multigrain Cheerios** (the multigrain ones in the purple & white box are the same the Original in the UK)
- Shreddies – **Cascadian Farm Multi Grain Squares**

Preserves section
- Fruit jelly (*jam*) – **Bonne Maman**
- Peanut Butter – **Smucker's Natural Chunky or Creamy**
- Honey
- Raisins – **Sunmaid**

Household Section
- Toilet paper
- Kitchen paper (*kitchen roll*)
- Saran wrap (*cling film*)
- Dish soap (*washing up liquid*) and/or dishwasher tablets

18 – RECREATING YOUR UK STORE CUPBOARD

You have probably had a chance to find your feet for a few days by now, but are finding your culinary choices somewhat limited by the absence of a well-stocked store cupboard. Now is the time to invest in a selection of basics to widen your dinner repertoire! Items marked with an * will probably/possibly be found in the International section. **Bold** indicates suggested brands. *Italics* indicates UK equivalent. Be prepared to shop around to get all of these items. You may need to visit a variety of stores to get everything you need.

Store cupboard basics
- Baking powder – **Rumford; Clabber Girl**
- Bicarbonate soda – **Arm & Hammer**
- Breadcrumbs – **Kikkoman Panko**
- Cornstarch (*cornflour*) – **Clabber Girl**
- Flour, all-purpose (*plain*) – **Gold Medal**
- Flour, self-rising (*self raising*)– **Gold Medal**
- Gravy – **Bisto***

- Herbs, dried:
    - Bay leaves
    - Italian herb mix (*mixed herbs*)
    - Oregano
    - Parsley
    - Rosemary
    - Sage
    - Thyme
- Oil, olive
- Oil, canola (*rapeseed oil*)
- Salt
- Spices:
    - Black pepper
    - Cayenne powder
    - Chili powder
    - Cinnamon
    - Cloves
    - Cumin
    - Curry powder
    - Five spice
    - Ginger
    - Nutmeg
    - Paprika
    - Pumpkin Spice Mix (*mixed spice*)
    - Turmeric
- Stock cubes/bouillon, chicken, beef & vegetable – **Knorr; Better Than Bouillon; Oxo***
- Stuffing – **Paxo***
- Sugar, cane (*granulated sugar*)
- Sugar, superfine cane (*caster sugar*)
- Sugar, confectioner's (*icing sugar*)
- Sugar, soft brown
- Vanilla extract
- Vinegar, malt – **Crosse & Blackwell, Sarson's***
- Vinegar, wine and/or balsamic

Grains & beans

- Couscous
- Lentils
- Oats
- Pasta, spirals/shapes
- Pasta, spaghetti
- Pearl Barley *
- Rice, instant
- Rice, Arborio or other risotto

Sauces & condiments

- BBQ Sauce
- Brown sauce – **HP***
- Curry paste – **Patak's***
- Fruit jelly (*jam*) – **Bonne Maman**
- Honey
- Ketchup – **Heinz Simply Heinz**
- Mayonnaise – **Hellmann's**
- Mustard, English – **Colman's***
- Mustard, wholegrain
- Peanut Butter
- Salad dressing, vinaigrette
- Salad Cream – **Heinz***
- Soy sauce – **Kikkoman***
- Teriyaki sauce – **Kikkoman***
- Tomato paste (*tomato puree*)
- Worcestershire Sauce – **Lea & Perrins**

INDEX

NOTES

ABOUT THE AUTHOR

Maxine Cleminson is a stay at home Mummy (or whatever the PC job title is these days)to 3 scrumptious little boys that keep her ~~crazy~~ ~~hectic~~ ~~infuriated~~ ~~loved up~~ busy but also inspire a lot of her ideas. Prior to children she was a senior school geography teacher; a beloved vocation, and a career she intends to return to when her kids are older.

She has written a regular blog called A Mama With Ideas (www.mamawithideas.com) since 2011, showcasing a wide range of her craft projects, recipes, organisation and parenting ideas, plus a lot of commentary about the expat lifestyle.

Maxine is originally from the south of England, but has lived in Houston, Texas since 2010. The experience of relocating to the USA planted the seed of an idea that has culminated in this book, her first. Something to tick off her bucket list!

3501670R00072

Printed in Great Britain
by Amazon.co.uk, Ltd.,
Marston Gate.